CRAFTY
FRENCH
COOKING

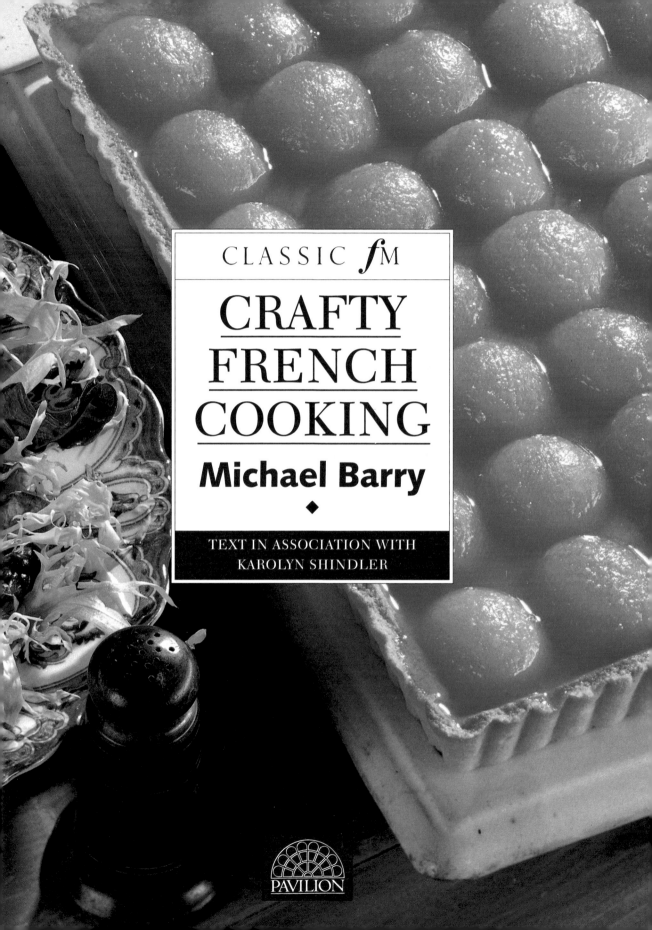

CLASSIC *f*M

CRAFTY
FRENCH
COOKING

Michael Barry

◆

TEXT IN ASSOCIATION WITH
KAROLYN SHINDLER

PAVILION

In the compilation of this book I would like to express my gratitude for the hard work of
Karolyn Shindler. In helping to research and compile the recipes and notes she has made a
valuable and substantial contribution.

First published in Great Britain in 1995 by
Pavilion Books Limited
26 Upper Ground
London SE1 9PD

🌿 Indicates recipes suitable for vegetarians

Designed by Andrew Barron & Collis Clements Associates

ISBN 1-85793-678 7

Typeset in Transitional 511 BT by Dorchester Typesetting Group Ltd.
Printed and bound in Italy by Graphicom

2 4 6 8 10 9 7 5 3 1

This book may be ordered by post direct from the publisher.
Please contact the Marketing Department. But try your bookshop first

Images on pages 2–3: Salad of Scallops and Asparagus (page 128), Apricot Tart (page 134)

CONTENTS

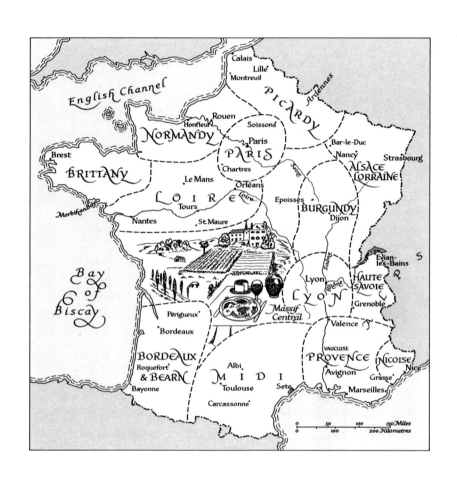

English Channel

Calais
Lille
Montreuil

PICARDY

Ardennes

Rouen
Honfleur
Soissons

NORMANDY
Paris
PARIS

Bar-le-Duc
Nancy

Strasbourg

ALSACE
LORRAINE

Brest

BRITTANY

Chartres

Le Mans
Orléans

LOIRE
Tours

Nantes
St. Maure

Morbihan Bay

Seine

Loire

Epoisses

BURGUNDY
Dijon

Evian-
les-Bains

Lyon

HAUTE
SAVOIE

Grenoble

Massif
Central

Valence

Bay
of
Biscay

Périgueux
Bordeaux

BORDEAUX
& BEARN
Roquefort
Bayonne

Albi

MIDI
Toulouse

Carcassonne

VAUCLUSE

PROVENCE

NICOISE
Nice

Avignon
Grasse

Sete
Marseilles

50   100   150 Miles
100   200 Kilometres

6

INTRODUCTION

Welcome to a cook's tour of France. For all the years I have been travelling to France, since I was eight years old, the country and the food have held a particular fascination for me. France is a huge and – by British standards – almost empty country. The intelligence, diligence and culture of its people, the magnificence of its cities and the wonderful collections of art and architecture that fill them, have always been a source of great joy. But at the heart of it all, I have to admit that the food of France has always been the sheet anchor of my delight in the country. I hope now to share some of that pleasure with you in this very personal tour.

This book does not attempt to look comprehensively at French regional cooking. Indeed, there are some quite substantial regions left out altogether, or mentioned only in passing. Nor does it try to cover all the cooking of those regions I do include, partly for reasons of space, partly because this is essentially a *crafty* cook's tour – one which selects the dishes and flavours, ingredients and combinations that are good in their own right but that also travel well to our supermarkets, shops and kitchens. We are lucky in that respect, as these days the range of French produce available in Britain is quite extraordinary, reflecting our fascination with the food of the Mediterranean. It is still not possible, however, to find a butcher who can cut meat in the French style, or to buy melons and peaches at quite the same level of scented perfection as those found for sale on any roadside in Provence. Essentially, I hope this book will give you a flavour of France without requiring that you follow all the formal or regional techniques or use the specific ingredients that are sometimes called for. In this, I am bound to say, I follow a lot of French domestic cooks who, like us, are often employed out of the house as well as in it, and for whom convenience cooking is extremely important. In fact, convenience has always been a major part of French cuisine, with the wonderful *traiteurs* and *pâtissiers* and *charcutiers* providing first and last courses of marvellous quality. In addition there are wonderful breads, cheeses and other ready-prepared dishes and ingredients to enjoy. But the French have not yet gone quite so far down the chill-cook route as we have, and at least one dish in any meal is likely to be properly prepared using fresh ingredients. The techniques, however, are often labour-saving, and it is that new style that I have tried to reflect, along with some of the more traditional dishes.

In choosing dishes from each of the regions, I have made a very personal choice. From the first time I tasted carrot soup in a tiny hotel in Brittany, aged eight, to a recent formal meal in the kitchens of one of the great hotels of Paris, individual dishes have always coloured my understanding of what makes up good regional French food. I hope I have reflected the produce and nature of the regions, and the kind of food enjoyed by the people who live there. Occasionally I may have left out what seems like a central dish, or one which you personally may have enjoyed when travelling. In that case I am sorry, but I hope you will nevertheless join me in enjoying some of the most varied cuisine in the world. France is not only a large country but also one of very different climates and traditions. From the cold northern European fields of Flanders to the sunbaked hills of the South, the produce and cooking vary enormously. But all of the dishes seem to pay particular attention to detail, with the subtle combination and balance of flavours and textures that make French food special – the benchmark against which we measure all other cuisines and styles of eating.

We enjoyed our radio tour around the provinces of France on Classic FM, and my host Henry Kelly turned out to be as much of a Francophile as so many of his Irish compatriots. Many of the recipes in this book appeared in that series, but there are others too – specially researched and always enjoyed. You may want to make sure that a meal balances in terms of richness, texture and flavour, so don't be afraid to choose dishes that come from different provinces – even in Paris food preparation and presentation has been drawn from all the provinces and mixed and matched according to personal taste.

We have included as well, in each chapter, a little note on the cheeses of the region, since these form an inevitable part of any French meal. In France cheeses are always eaten after the main course and before the pudding as they are held to be a savoury rather than a sweet contribution to the meal. They are also eaten with bread rather than with biscuits, though in this, as in all things, you must suit yourself. I hope that you enjoy this crafty tour of the cooking of France as much as I have enjoyed preparing it.

Fromage de France

FRENCH CHEESE

Cheese is one of the great wonders of France – and one of its biggest industries. Cheese-making itself goes back thousands of years, and some French cheeses have a clear, honourable and delicious history! There are literally hundreds of cheeses made in France, produced from goats', ewes' and cows' milk. As the quality of much of French wine is guaranteed by the *Appellation Contrôlée* (AC) label, so some French cheeses have a similar status. At the moment there are 32 cheeses entitled to what is called *Appellation d'Origine Contrôlée* (AOC) status, which guarantees that the cheese has been made where it should have been made, that specific production and ripening processes have been followed, that the cheese has traditional qualities and characteristics and that strict control procedures have been followed. The list on the right are AOC cheeses.

Although the quality of all these traditional cheeses is guaranteed, there are also many other marvellous cheeses available in France and in specialist shops here which are quite wonderful and the genuine article, but do not have AOC status because they are perhaps relatively new, or only produced in small quantities or for other good reasons which have nothing to do with their quality.

HOW TO PUT TOGETHER A CHEESEBOARD

When you're putting together a cheeseboard, you need to think of flavour, intensity and texture. You need a balance of cheeses and not too many. Four is probably enough, with a balance of texture, so you have some that are firm and some that are creamy. You also need a balance of intensity, so you need some that are mild and meadow-like, and some that have a loud almost explosive flavour. To put names to them, you could have perhaps, a smooth creamy Brie, the firm flavoured and textured Pont l'Eveque, a distinctive goat cheese, say a cendre, which is one of my favourites, and lastly for its explosive quality on the tongue, the great Roquefort. But each region of France has its own distinctive cheeses, which are well worth exploring. Whatever cheeses you choose, eat them with grapes, ripe pears and a little French bread, rather than biscuits.

Cows' milk

Abondance

Beaufort

Bleu d'Auvergne

Bleu des Causses

Bleu de Gex or du Haut Jura

Brie de Meaux

Brie de Melun

Camembert de Normandie

Cantel

Chaource

Comté

Epoisses de Bourgogne

Fourme d'Ambert or de Montbrison

Laguiole

Langres

Livarot

Maroilles

Mont d'Or or Vacherin du Haut-Doubs

Munster

Neufchâtel

Pont-l'Eveque

Reblochon

Saint-Nectaire

Salers

Goats' milk

Chabichou du Poitou

Crottin de Chavignol

Picoden de l'Ardèche or de la Drôme

Pouligny Saint-Pierre

Sainte-Maure de Touraine

Selles-sur-Cher

Sheeps milk

Ossau-Iraty-Brebis-Pyrénées

Roquefort

PROVENCE

South of Valence and and east of the Rhône lies Provence. The very name reveals its origins. It is named for the 'Provincia Romana', the first of the many places Rome conquered as it expanded its empire, and the one it held on to for longest, adjacent as it is to Italy and the ancient trade route along the Mediterranean coast. The name also excites the most fervent passions, and for the last century – from the time when Escoffier admired the asparagus of the region to the recent success of the Mayle books – the region has been a fantasy of sun-kissed plenty to the English. Its cooking has also been inspirational. Elizabeth David, the great re-inventor of good food for us British after the last war, once described the food of Provence as 'the rational, right and proper food for human beings to eat'. Provençal food, of course, reflects the region's history and its location – an area fought over almost continually from the fall of the Roman Empire until the middle of the nineteenth century. It was subject to a wide range of influences – Italian, North African, French – and was one of the first places in northern Europe to embrace the ingredients of the New World. Peppers and tomatoes are now synonymous with the region and its cooking.

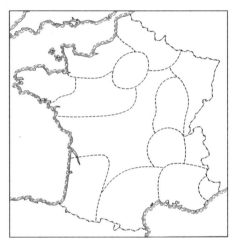

Provençal food very much reflects the climate of the region. In winter, Provence can be cold and even bleak, with the Mistral wind blowing for weeks at a time. Because of this, the cuisine includes daubes, rich southern casseroles, fish stews and rice dishes from the Camargue at the mouth of the Rhône. But it is really summer food that we think of as Provençal: ripe, light dishes of salads and tomatoes; the grills and fish flavoured with olives and olive oil. In every little market town – indeed, in every little stall in every little farmyard – you can buy vegetables and fruit of a ripeness and quality achieved nowhere else in Europe: the tomatoes are large, often slightly misshapen, dark red and good enough to eat either on their own in thick slices or with some crusty bread; peaches and nectarines abound – white-fleshed, golden-fleshed, smooth-skinned, furry-skinned – all succulent and dripping with juice; black and green figs; grapes with that special scented Muscat flavour that the South specializes in; and aubergines, peppers, courgettes, olives in vivid heaps. The oil of Provence – the dark green, pungent olive oil – is typical too, and is used for cooking and dressing salads, and even for protecting the skin from the rays of the sun.

Opposite: Lavender fields in Provence.

Nearer the coast, fish has always been a speciality, although these days the number of people who live and holiday there has made the fish both scarce and fiercely expensive. Even so, salted or tinned anchovies appear in many of the dishes, and there are still enough sardines to make them a favourite on the waterfront – delicious when freshly grilled and served with no more than a pinch of salt and a slice of lemon. Away from the coast, countless villages perch up in the hills – often at the very top of the incline, making them lovely to look at but difficult to get to. It is in these villages, and in their larger cousins, that some of the other specialities of Provence become apparent: honeys and jams and jellies, particularly near the town of Apt; the perfumed sweets from the town of Grasse; truffles from Vaucluse; and each speciality is often presented on the lovely white-based, flower-painted pottery of the region.

When visiting Provence these days, especially in high summer, it is worth being wary of so-called specialities like *bouillabaisse*, originally a fisherman's soup made with the leftover, unsaleable bony fish. It is now in such demand that it is often not as good as it might be. Look out instead for the less expensive but often better-made *soupe de poissons* that is also served with croûtons, cheese and rouille (the garlic and chilli-flavoured mayonnaise of Provence). Jams and honeys are always worth buying and bringing home, since they preserve the distinct flavours and memories of summer days. Wines, by and large, travel less well and tend to be whites or rosés. It's not a cheese country really, either, although there are a number of goats' cheeses which have an outstanding flavour and reputation, in particular Banon, little mild cheeses often wrapped prettily in chestnut leaves and bound with straw.

The last word about Provence – perhaps most central of all – should be devoted to herbs. Wherever you go in summer the smell of herbs is always there, for they grow wild on the rocky hillsides: lavender, thyme, rosemary and – if you're lucky – basil. They scent the air in markets too, and in the kitchens, where they are used with a more generous hand than anywhere else in France. Rosemary with lamb, basil with tomato, thyme with the rich beef stews flavoured with orange peel and, surprisingly, with lavender too. It is the scented air more than the intensity of light that marks the pleasure that is Provence.

Soupe de Poisson Provençale
PROVENÇAL FISH SOUP

Fish soup in France is simply part of life; North, West or here in the South, fish soups are made using the best of wonderful local ingredients. Some soups, like the traditional method of cooking bouillabaisse, can be difficult and time-consuming requiring 17 different kinds of fish – though there are delicious and simpler variations. But on a recent visit to France, I found this recipe, which is a lovely, modern-style fish soup, based on fish stock. You can make the stock yourself, from fish trimmings, lemon and bay leaves, or you can now buy it ready-made in jars, frozen in tubs, or in stock cubes.

Peel the onions, cut the ends off the courgettes and take the seeds and white bits out of the peppers. Cut these and the tomatoes into pieces about the size of a walnut. In a large frying pan or saucepan, heat the olive oil and fry the vegetables for 2 or 3 minutes until they are just starting to brown. Season generously and add the fish stock. Simmer for no more than 10 minutes – this is a very light and delicate soup – until the vegetables are just cooked through.

Put the whole lot either through a *mouli-légume* – a sort of sieve with a handle to wind things through it – or pour the soup into a liquidizer and give it a quick whizz. The soup is now a delicate, pale gold, flecked with the colours of the vegetables – pale green and bright red. Add the lemon juice, but taste the soup first: how much lemon you need depends on how much was in the fish stock to start with. Check for seasoning. Float a slice of French bread on to each serving, top with a tablespoon of rouille, and sprinkle the grated Gruyère cheese, fennel or dill leaves on top of that.

Serves 4

175g/6oz each onions, courgettes, red or green peppers and tomatoes

1 tablespoon olive oil

Salt and freshly ground black pepper

900ml/1½ pints fish stock

Juice of ½ lemon

4 slices lightly toasted French bread

4 tablespoons Rouille (see p.16)

4 tablespoons grated Gruyère cheese

A few fresh fennel or dill leaves or 1 teaspoon freeze-dried fennel or dill

Soupe au Pistou
SOUP WITH PISTOU

Pistou is the Provençal equivalent of the Italian pesto – a wonderful, fragrant concoction of fresh basil leaves, olive oil and cheese. The soup itself is a close cousin of minestrone – a *mélange* of dried haricot or flageolet beans, tomatoes and vegetables. It is one of the best dishes that I know to warm up a cold day, but because of the marvellous summery tastes, it makes a perfect single dish meal at any time of year. Simply follow it with bread, cheese and fruit.

Serves 4

For the soup:

175g/6oz dried haricot or flageolet beans

1 large onion, 1 large courgette and 1 leek

225g/8oz each new potatoes and little green stringless beans

Provençal Fish Soup
(page 13)
Chicken Riviera
(page 18)

2 stalks celery

100g/4oz carrots

2 large tomatoes

50g/2oz soup pasta – small shells or little macaroni

For the pistou:

25g/1oz fresh basil leaves

2 cloves garlic, peeled

1 large tomato, halved and with the seeds scooped out

2 tablespoons olive oil

50g/2oz grated Gruyère cheese

Salt and freshly ground black pepper

The dried haricot or flageolet beans must be soaked in water for 6 hours before use – or follow the instructions on the packet. At the end of the soaking time, drain them, rinse well and bring them to the boil in lots of water and simmer for 1½ hours until tender. Peel the onion, potatoes and carrots, trim the green beans, courgette, leek and celery and chop all the vegetables, including the tomatoes, into 1cm/½ inch dice. Put the green beans and tomatoes to one side, and put all the other vegetables and the cooked haricot or flageolet beans into a large pan with 1.2 litres/2 pints/5 cups of water and 1 teaspoon of salt. Bring to the boil, turn down the heat and simmer for 15 minutes until the vegetables are cooked through but have not disintegrated. Add the pasta, the tomatoes and the green beans, simmer for another 3 minutes, then turn off the heat, put on the saucepan lid and leave the soup to stand for about 10 minutes.

To make the pistou, put the basil, garlic, tomato, olive oil and grated Gruyère into a food processor or liquidizer and process until puréed. Season with salt and pepper.

To serve, stir a tablespoon of the pistou into the saucepan, then ladle the soup into individual bowls. Serve the rest of the pistou in a separate dish so people can add it at their own discretion! You can also serve a separate bowl of grated Gruyère and lots of hot crusty French bread.

HOW TO MAKE ROUILLE

For mayonnaise:

1 egg, preferably at room temperature

3–4 tablespoons olive oil

½ teaspoon each salt and sugar

Juice of ½ lemon

7–8 tablespoons sunflower oil

For aïoli – garlic mayonnaise:

1 clove of garlic, peeled

For rouille:

1–2 teaspoons chilli sauce, according to taste

Rouille is an essential part of Provençal cuisine. It is a wonderful, rich, garlicky, spicily hot sauce, used for soups, fish and some meat dishes. You can buy it in jars in specialist shops or the larger supermarkets, but home-made rouille has a marvellous freshness and my Crafty way of making it is very easy. It can only be made, by this method, in a liquidizer or blender. You start by making a mayonnaise, which takes hardly any time or effort at all. When the clove of garlic is added it becomes aïoli, and when the chilli sauce is added, you have rouille.

Method:
To make the basic mayonnaise, break the egg into the blender or liquidizer and pour in the olive oil, salt, sugar and lemon juice. Process it briefly, then with the motor still running and the hole in the middle of the lid open, pour the sunflower oil into the mixture in a slow thin stream. Gradually it will blend in, and suddenly the mayonnaise will thicken and become shiny. Keep going until all the oil is used up. Scoop it out of the machine, and put it in a bowl or jar. It will keep in the fridge for up to a week.

To make garlic mayonnaise – aïoli:
Proceed as for mayonnaise, adding to all the ingredients in the processor the peeled clove of garlic. Process until the garlic is puréed, then add the sunflower oil as in the method above.

To make rouille:
Add the chilli sauce to the aïoli so it turns pale pink and seriously pungent.

How to use rouille:
For each serving of Provençale Fish Soup (see p. 13), put 1 tablespoon of rouille on to a slice of lightly toasted French bread, and sprinkle the top with grated Gruyère cheese.

Salade aux Noix
SALAD WITH WALNUTS

I like to serve this marvellously flavoured salad either as a starter or after the main course. Walnut oil is fresh and nutty, though the taste is quite strong. Experiment a bit; you may prefer to dilute it slightly with a mild oil such as safflower. Once the bottle of walnut oil is open, keep it in the fridge; the freshness will be preserved much longer if you do.

Tear the salad leaves into pieces about half the size of a postcard. As you tear the leaves, you crush the veins closed and the liquid stays in the leaves. If you cut the leaves, you allow all the liquid to drain out and you are left with a soft and floppy salad. Wash and dry the salad leaves thoroughly, then put them into a big bowl. In a separate bowl, put the lemon juice, sugar and salt, and whisk thoroughly together until the sugar and salt have dissolved. Then add the 6 tablespoons of walnut oil. Whisk until it has all emulsified and is smooth and cloudy. Just before you are ready to eat, pour the dressing over the salad and toss thoroughly, then sprinkle the walnuts – which you have lightly crushed in your hand – over the top. You end up with a marvellous crunch, a bitter-sweet dressing and a fantastic nutty flavour.

Serves 4

Lettuce – frisée and radicchio, or any combination of leaves you happen to like

Juice of 1 lemon

1 teaspoon sugar

½ teaspoon salt

6 tablespoons walnut oil

50g/2oz shelled walnuts

Epaule d'Agneau Provençale
SHOULDER OF LAMB PROVENÇALE

I cooked a shoulder of lamb like this for a Sunday lunch in the South of France. When we rose from the table, not a morsel was left! It is a dish of wonderful, warm, summery flavours, very easy to do and meltingly tender. Frozen New Zealand lamb is excellent for this – it is well hung with a very good rich flavour. But if good English or Welsh lamb is available, then that will also do very well.

If the lamb is frozen, let it thaw overnight. Trim and prepare the courgettes, aubergines, onions, tomatoes and peppers, and cut them all into quite small dice, about 1cm/½ inch across. Mix them together and put them into a large casserole or, best of all, an oval roaster, together with the olive oil and garlic. Heat it on top of the stove for a few minutes, just until it starts to sizzle a bit. Put the trimmed lamb on top of the vegetables, the rosemary on the lamb and season the whole lot generously. Put the lid on and cook in a medium oven at 180°C/160°C fan/350°F/Gas Mark 4,

Serves 6

1 whole shoulder of lamb, about 1.75kg/4lb

225g/8oz each aubergines, courgettes, onions and tomatoes – preferably big French beef tomatoes

100g/4oz each red and green peppers

4 tablespoons olive oil

1 clove garlic, peeled

Sprig of fresh rosemary

Salt and freshly ground black pepper

or the bottom of an Aga roasting oven, for 45 minutes per kg/ 20 minutes per lb, plus 20 minutes. So if the leg of lamb weighs 1.75kg/4lb, it needs 1 hour and 40 minutes, and so on.

When it has cooked, the vegetables will be flavoured with the lamb, and the lamb will have absorbed the flavours of the vegetables. The meat will be unbelievably tender and easy to carve. Put a couple of tablespoons of the vegetables on each plate and top with generous portions of the lamb. There will be juices at the bottom of the casserole and you can pour them over the top. Pommes de Terre à l'Ail, roast potatoes flavoured with garlic (see p. 19) go perfectly with this.

Poulet Riviera
CHICKEN RIVIERA

Serves 4

1 chicken, about
1.5–1.75kg/3–4lb

2 tablespoons oil

2 cloves garlic, peeled
and chopped

Juice of 1 lemon

450g/1lb scrubbed new
potatoes

450g/1lb cherry
tomatoes

1 teaspoon freeze-dried
basil

1 tablespoon chopped
fresh parsley

Tomatoes in southern France are a treat in themselves – warm from the sun, rich and red. This recipe captures some of that flavour, even though those big French tomatoes, curiously, seem to travel least successfully of all fruit and vegetables. Little, sweet baby tomatoes do very well in this dish. They are added at the last moment, so although they are hot, they are still firm and juicy. If you can possibly avoid it, don't use a frozen chicken – the full flavour of a fresh free-range chicken is worth the extra expense. Slightly cheaper are the French maize-fed chickens, which many supermarkets now sell. They have a light golden tinge to their flesh from the corn.

You need an ovenproof casserole which will also go on top of the stove for this. Heat the oil in the casserole and brown the chicken on all sides. Put the garlic into the casserole, pour the lemon juice over the chicken, put the lid on, and bake in a medium oven at 180°C/160°C fan/350°F/Gas Mark 4, or the middle of an Aga roasting oven, for 40 minutes.

Cut the potatoes into small dice – about 1cm/½ inch – and add to the casserole. Continue to bake the chicken for another 25 minutes, and check to make sure it is thoroughly cooked by pushing a skewer or fork into the thickest part of the leg. The juices should run clear. If they are still pink, continue cooking for another 10 minutes and test again. Then add the cherry tomatoes, arranging them in the casserole around the chicken, sprinkle the basil over the top, and cook for another 5 minutes or so until the tomatoes are just heated through. When you are ready to serve, the bright green of the chopped fresh parsley scattered over the top looks marvellous against the red of the tomatoes and golden brown of the chicken.

Topinambours à la Provençale
JERUSALEM ARTICHOKES PROVENÇALE

I love the crisp texture of Jerusalem artichokes and their lovely hazelnutty flavour which combines marvellously with the tomato and garlic flavours of southern France. Jerusalem artichokes used to be quite fiddly to deal with because they needed to be peeled. These days, the new varieties just need to be scrubbed. If you can find sundried tomato purée, do use it. It has a marvellous, rich, deep flavour, perfect for this recipe.

Crush the garlic clove with the salt. Scrub the artichokes, pat them dry and cut them into 5mm/¼ inch slices. Heat the oil in a large frying pan and sauté the artichokes for 5 minutes on each side. Stir in the onion and garlic salt, then add the tomato purée, the capers and just enough water to make the dish moist, but not runny. Cook over a gentle heat, stirring occasionally, for 20–25 minutes until the sauce is really thick. Stir the artichokes through the sauce so they are coated evenly. I like this as a dish on its own, but it also makes a very good side dish with grilled meat or fish.

Serves 4 as a starter or side dish, 2 as a main course

1 clove garlic, peeled

1 teaspoon salt

450g/1lb Jerusalem artichokes

2 tablespoons olive oil

1 onion, peeled and finely chopped

2 tablespoons sundried tomato purée

1 teaspoon capers

Pommes de Terre à l'Ail
ROAST POTATOES WITH GARLIC

The addition of garlic and parsley and olive oil to these potatoes evokes warmth, sunshine and the *bonhomie* of warmer climes. This is a dish I first ate in a restaurant in southern France, since when it has become one of my favourite ways of roasting potatoes. It goes wonderfully with Épaule d'Agneau Provençale (see p. 17) – and countless other dishes which are based on the southern flavours of olive oil and herbs.

Put the potatoes into a saucepan of cold water and bring to the boil. Cook for just 5 minutes, no more, and drain them immediately. In a roasting tin, heat the olive oil with the garlic. The idea is not to cover the potatoes with garlic, but to flavour the oil with it. When the oil is really hot, roll the drained potatoes in the garlicky oil so they are thoroughly coated.

Let them bake in a medium oven at 180°C/160°C fan/350°F/Gas Mark 4, or a bit higher, or in the top of an Aga roasting oven while the joint is cooking, for at least 40–60 minutes. You'll need to turn them at least once. The potatoes should be crisp and golden, flavoured with the garlicky oil. When you're ready to serve them, take them out, put

Serves 4

900g/2lb/10 medium potatoes, peeled and cut into even-sized pieces

6 tablespoons olive oil

2 cloves garlic, peeled and halved

Salt and freshly ground black pepper

A handful chopped fresh parsley

them on a serving dish, sprinkle with a little salt and pepper and the handful of chopped parsley. That adds a marvellous brightness and greenness to the dish. The Pommes de Terre à l'Ail and the Shoulder of Lamb Provençale together make the most sublimely delicious lunch!

Salade d'Épinards
SPINACH SALAD

Serves 4 as a main course, 8 as a starter or side salad

450g/1lb spinach leaves – buy the ready prepared baby spinach if you can

Salt and freshly ground black pepper

1 tablespoon runny honey

1 tablespoon lemon juice

2 tablespoons oil – sunflower or safflower

For the croûtons:

2 slices wholemeal bread

1–2 tablespoons oil

1 teaspoon mixed herbs – preferably Herbes Provençales

A salad made of small, crisp fresh spinach leaves of a deep, rich green is one of my great delights, particularly if it is eaten in the warmth of the Provençal sun, gazing at the Mediterranean! On a hot day, this is the perfect salad for lunch, served on its own with just some warm crusty French bread – which you could try dipped in the best olive oil, rather than spread with butter.

To make the croûtons, cut the bread into small cubes of about 5mm/¼ inch and fry them in a little oil until pale gold. Sprinkle with the herbs. Wash and dry the spinach well if you haven't bought it ready prepared, and tear the leaves into pieces about 2.5cm/1 inch across (about the size of 50p coins). Season generously with salt and pepper. Gently heat the honey and lemon juice together in a saucepan until the honey melts. Then add the oil, stir, and when the dressing is hot, pour it over the spinach and serve at once with the croûtons sprinkled over the top.

Melon aux Raisins
MELON BASKET WITH GRAPES

Serves 4

2 Galia melons

225g/8oz seedless grapes, assorted red and green

This is a simple and beautiful pudding, very fresh and sweet.

With a sharp knife, cut round the equator of the melon by pushing in the knife in a series of interlocked gentle stabs with the knife held at an angle of 45 degrees, so the marks round the melon appear to be saw-toothed. When you have gone all the way round, the melon will pull apart into 2 halves with a neat zigzag edge on each half. Scoop out the seeds and trim the base of the melons so they sit neatly as dishes. Wash the grapes and remove from the stalks. Mix them together for colour and pile into the melon bowls. Chill and serve.

Salade de Pêches
PEACH SALAD

One of the greatest pleasures of Provence is wandering round the markets – which are really where you decide what you are going to eat that day! The quality of the fruit is astonishing, and in the summer the stalls are as full of succulent, delicate white peaches as they are of the golden variety. If you can find white peaches here, they are well worth the extra expense as the flavour is so much more sweet and intense.

Dip the peaches into a bowl of boiling water for about 10–15 seconds. You'll find the skins will slip off easily. Cut the peaches in half and remove the stones. The crafty way of doing this is to treat them like an avocado. Cut a line all the way round the peach with a sharp knife, and, using a bit of kitchen paper, gently twist the 2 halves as if you were unscrewing them. You'll find one half will come off and the stone will come out of the other half. Cut each half into slices.

In a separate bowl, mix the caster sugar and the lemon juice. Sprinkle the lemon rind on to the peaches. When the caster sugar has dissolved in the lemon juice, mix that in with the peach slices and leave to marinate in the fridge for at least 2 hours. The flavour of the lemon just penetrates the sweetness of the peaches and produces a marvellous combination. Just before you serve the salad, tear up some fresh mint leaves, stir a few into the salad and sprinkle the rest on top. The mint adds a fresh green scent and taste to this lovely peach salad.

Serves 4

4 large peaches, white peaches if you can find them

1 tablespoon caster sugar

Juice of 1 lemon

Grated rind of ½ lemon

Sprigs of fresh mint

PROVENÇAL CHEESEBOARD

The warm Provençal sun produces strong, idiosyncratic cheeses, made from ewes', cows' and goats' milk. Many are marvellous, memorable cheeses, but they do not really travel well. To put together a Provençal cheeseboard in this country could be tricky, as so few are widely available, but you can add to the real thing 2 or 3 of the stronger goats' cheeses which most supermarkets now stock.

The Provençal cheese you can buy here is Banon. Depending on the time of year, it can be made from all 3 types of milk. It is often wrapped in chestnut leaves and steeped in a local *marc*. The texture is soft and the flavour can be sweet or nutty. Poivre d'âne, the French equivalent of savory, is sometimes used to flavour it.

In Provence itself, Picodon is well worth seeking out. It is a goats' cheese, small and round with a soft centre and a crust which varies from a bluish colour to red or gold, depending on its ripeness. Picodon de l'Ardèche or de la Drôme have AOC status.

PARIS

Paris forms the centre of France in a way no British person can really understand. It is in fact where France originated, the area around the city being called the Île de France. In medieval times it was often the only piece of land the French kings controlled, as first the British and then the Burgundians swept across the countryside. Nevertheless, from this time onwards the wealth of France, and indeed of much of Europe, flowed towards Paris. By the beginning of the eighteenth century it had become the artistic and cultural capital of the western world, a position it has struggled to maintain – with varying degrees of success – for almost 300 years.

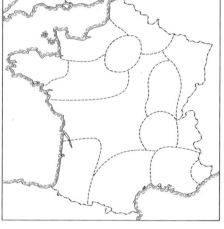

Paris has always been an amalgam of culinary styles, and the incredible range of the area's natural resources is reflected in the names of the food: foamy whipped cream from Chantilly – also the name of the lace that echoes its delicacy; Paris mushrooms cultivated in the granite quarries from which the building blocks of Paris were taken, and which have given their name to the commercial mainstay of mushroom growing throughout Europe; the cherries of Montmorency to the east of the city; and the great wheat fields around Chartres which, together with the market gardens of Soissons, supply some of the finest produce in the whole of France.

Shopping for food in Paris is a difficult but pleasurable task. You find yourself torn between the local shops, which sell meat, breads, pastries and groceries, and the city's wonderful markets. Both the retail markets, which abound in small squares and shopping streets on the periphery of the city, and the great early-morning wholesale market, which has replaced Les Halles, are full of delicious temptations. In addition there are speciality food shops in the centre of the city. The most famous of these is the beautiful but expensive Fauchon on the edge of the Place de la Concorde – worth a visit even if you only buy a small bottle of flavoured vinegar or a tiny tin of perfumed sweets. The experience of looking and smelling can take up a totally absorbing morning.

Domestic cooking in Paris can be of a superb standard, especially the bourgeois traditions maintained in homes throughout the city and its hinterland, but the city's true speciality can be found in its restaurants. Some, like Pruniers and the Tour d'Argent, have been famous for generations; others emerge new and flourish, then fail

Opposite: The typical Parisian sight of the Métro station.

23

again, but there always remains a core of excellent three-star restaurants which continue to thrive. The food served in Parisian restaurants has changed dramatically with the fashions, but never more so than in the last fifteen years, when nouvelle cuisine – lighter food, elegantly presented in ever more exotic combinations – has swept the board. But over the same period there has been a quite different trend taking place at the bottom end of the trade. Like all great capitals, Paris attracts people seeking their fortune from the provinces and from the country's overseas associates such as the French-speaking parts of Africa, the West Indies and Asia. As a result brasseries specializing in the food of Alsace-Lorraine, the Béarn, Tunisia and Vietnam have sprung up, offering good food and great value for money. It's also worth looking for establishments in the suburbs, the *faubourgs*, of Paris. These restaurants *de quartier* are the backbone of eating out for Parisians: with their fixed menus and competitive prices they represent those aspects of French cooking that have made the cuisine legendary.

It might sometimes appear that there are more guide books than restaurants in Paris, but it is worth looking for the occasional restaurant that specializes in very old-fashioned French food: those offering a restricted menu and a long history, coupled with a loyal clientele, can often be found in the back streets rather than under the bright lights. Years ago, a food expert wrote, 'Nowhere in the world can one eat as well as one still does in Paris.' I suspect that, if you take a little trouble to find your way around, you will find that comment is still true today.

Soupe à l'Oignon
FRENCH ONION SOUP

The greatest of all the Parisian traditions is the onion soup which was eaten at Les Halles, the famous fruit and vegetable market – very similar to Covent Garden in London. Most cookery writers tell how they first tasted it in Les Halles when they were young. Unfortunately, they were pulling the market down by the time *I* got there, but the recipe is incredible. It was eaten not only by the market porters, who swore by its restorative powers as they toiled away all night, but also by the revellers of *la vie Parisienne* who probably ate it for much the same reason!

Heat the oil and butter or dripping in a large, solid saucepan. Fry the onions gently for about 15 minutes, stirring occasionally, until they are a rich brown, but not burnt. Add the sugar and stir continuously for 3–4 minutes. The sugar acts to caramelize the onions and turns them a golden, rich brown. Turn the heat up slightly if the onions seem slow to brown, but do not let them burn! Add the garlic and season generously, then pour in the stock. Bring the soup to the boil and let it simmer, uncovered, very gently for at least 35 minutes, stirring occasionally. The onions will almost melt into the soup, but will still have a texture of their own.

To serve, ladle the soup into heatproof bowls, float a slice of the French bread on top and heap on each the grated Gruyère cheese. Put the bowls under a very hot grill for a minute or two until the cheese bubbles and melts.

Serves 6

2 tablespoons oil

100g/4oz butter or beef dripping

1.25kg/2½lb onions, peeled and thinly sliced

1 dessertspoon granulated sugar

1 clove garlic, peeled and chopped

Salt and freshly ground black pepper

1.2l/2 pints good beef stock, home-made, frozen or a good stock cube

4 slices French bread

100g/4oz grated Gruyère cheese

Pâté de Pigeon
PIGEON PÂTÉ

Pigeon has a marvellous, rich taste and quite a dense texture. It is widely available – in fact quite a few supermarkets now stock it. It is also the cheapest game available. There are lots of recipes which require just the breast of the pigeon, and pigeon pâté is a great way of using up the rest of the bird. The intensity of its flavour means you don't really need much pigeon meat for this recipe.

If you have a food processor or liquidizer, pour all the ingredients into it and process until smooth. Otherwise, mince the pigeon meat and chicken livers and stir in the rest of the ingredients. Spoon the mixture into a mould or soufflé dish, smooth the top and decorate with a few juniper berries. Put the dish into a baking tin and make a *bain marie* by pouring water into the tin until it comes halfway up the side of the dish. Bake in a medium oven

Serves 4

100g/4oz pigeon meat

225g/8oz chicken livers, washed

1 egg

¼ teaspoon ground allspice

¼ teaspoon each thyme and parsley

Salt and freshly ground black pepper

A few juniper berries for decoration

at 180°C/160°C fan/350°F/Gas Mark 4, or the bottom of the Aga, for 45 minutes. You can cover the top of the pâté with silver foil if it looks likely to burn. Allow to cool, then chill in the fridge for at least 4 hours before serving.

Boeuf Parisienne
PARISIAN BEEF

Serves 4

450g/1lb cold roast beef in thin slices

1 bunch spring onions, trimmed and finely chopped

1 teaspoon finely chopped celery leaf (optional)

3 tablespoons finely chopped fresh parsley

½ quantity vinaigrette dressing (see below)

Salt and freshly ground black pepper

Arrange the slices of beef on a great big serving platter and spread the chopped spring onions, celery leaf if you are using it, and the parsley over the top. Take the vinaigrette, make sure it is still amalgamated, and pour it carefully, spoonful by spoonful, over the beef. Leave it for half an hour or so to marinate, so the flavours penetrate the meat. Serve with hot new potatoes. It is just scrumtilious!

HOW TO MAKE VINAIGRETTE

2 tablespoons fresh lemon juice

2 tablespoons red wine vinegar or white wine or cider vinegar

1 teaspoon caster sugar

½ teaspoon salt

50ml/2fl oz olive oil

250ml/8fl oz sunflower or salad oil

Vinaigrette made properly is wonderful; made poorly, it can set your teeth on edge! The balance of oils is very much a matter of taste. I prefer to use a mixture of olive oil and salad oil, but you can use all salad oil for a lighter vinaigrette, or all olive oil for a stronger taste. Whichever you use, the total quantity of oil should measure 10fl oz, which is 300ml or 1¼ cups. The vinegar too is very important. Whatever you use, it should be a good one. Red wine vinegar is my preferred choice as a rule,

but white wine or cider vinegars are also fine. Don't, however, use malt vinegar! For a proper vinaigrette, the order you make it in is crucial, otherwise the ingredients just won't amalgamate properly.

Method:
In a screw-top jar, a food processor or a bowl with a whisk, mix together the lemon juice, vinegar, sugar and salt until the salt and sugar are thoroughly dissolved. Don't add the oil until this has happened. Then add both kinds of oil

and mix thoroughly. The vinaigrette is now ready for use, and any that is left over will keep happily in the fridge in a screw-top jar for up to 2 weeks.

How to use vinaigrette:
The French are much more adventurous than we are in their use of sauces and dressings. This vinaigrette is perfect for salads, but also for cold meats, such as the above dish, which is a favourite in Parisian brasseries.

Lapin Sauté aux Pruneaux et Jus de Raisin
RABBIT WITH PRUNES AND GRAPE JUICE

France produces some of the best prunes in the world, including a marvellous treat available here, which is prunes stuffed with prunes! The combination of the sweetness of prunes and the delicate flavour of rabbit is just delicious. It is often served with rice, but I like it with broad, flat noodles, such as tagliatelle.

Soak the prunes in the grape juice for at least 30 minutes and up to 2 hours before you begin to cook this. In a large pan, heat the oil and sauté the chopped garlic and rabbit pieces until golden. The rabbit will take about 5 minutes each side. Add the prunes and grape juice and simmer gently, uncovered, for about 30 minutes until the rabbit is tender and the prunes are plump. Make sure the liquid doesn't boil or you will have mushy prunes.

Stir the cornflour into the cream and add the lemon juice. The mixture will thicken quickly. Stir it spoonful by spoonful into the sauce in the pan and season generously. The balance of flavours should be just right: the lemon juice should balance the sweetness of the prunes and grape juice and the sauce should be thick and creamy.

Serves 4

175g/6oz prunes

300ml/10fl oz white grape juice

1 tablespoon oil

1 clove garlic, peeled and finely chopped

1 rabbit, jointed

2 teaspoons cornflour

150ml/5fl oz double cream

Juice of ½ lemon

Salt and freshly ground black pepper

Poulet Rôti à la Française
FRENCH ROAST CHICKEN

The French rear chickens with such a wonderful flavour that roast chicken appears on many of the best Parisian restaurant menus. Some of the finest come from just south of Burgundy in the district of Bresse. So good is the flavour that all they need is some butter and a little lemon to produce a sumptuous dish. It is difficult to find chickens from Bresse in this country, though you could use the French-reared chickens which are available here, particularly the golden corn-fed ones. I use free-range chickens, whenever possible, for their very good flavour and texture.

Put the half-lemon inside the chicken, with about a tablespoon of the butter. Put another spoonful of the butter into a shallow, oval gratin-type dish (a roasting tin will do), and put the chicken on its side on top of the butter. Rub the remaining spoonful of butter into the exposed side of the chicken and season with salt and pepper. Roast in a medium hot oven at 190°C/170°C fan/375°F/Gas Mark 5, or the middle of an Aga roasting oven for 45 minutes per kg/20 minutes per lb. After one-third of the

Serves 4

½ lemon, preferably unwaxed

1 roasting chicken, preferably free-range, about 1.5kg/3lb

3 tablespoons softened butter

Salt and freshly ground black pepper

2 tablespoons double cream (optional)

½ teaspoon freeze-dried thyme or tarragon (optional)

French Onion Soup
(page 25)

cooking time, turn the chicken over to its other side. Then, after the same amount of time, turn it again so the breast is uppermost. Baste the chicken each time you turn it.

At the end of the cooking time, test to see if the chicken is cooked by pushing a skewer into the thickest part of the leg. If the juices run clear, it's done. If they're still pink, cook for another 20 minutes and test again. Take the chicken out of the oven and let it rest in a warm place for 10 minutes before carving. The wonderful, buttery juices on their own make a marvellous sauce, but you can add to them in a saucepan the cream and a few herbs, with perhaps a little water to thin it down. Bring to the boil, stir, and serve with this succulent roast chicken.

Homard Thermidor
LOBSTER THERMIDOR

Serves 4

1 cooked and split lobster, about 900g/2lb

1 tablespoon Bordeaux or Dijon mustard

Salt and freshly ground black pepper

100g/4oz cup grated Gruyère cheese

For the Béchamel sauce:

200ml/7fl oz milk

2 tablespoons flour, sieved

25g/1oz butter

Pinch of freshly grated nutmeg

Salt

2 tablespoons double cream or fromage frais (optional)

Lobster is the most expensive and luxurious shellfish of all, with rich, dense white flesh. It is wonderful just boiled or grilled with lemon and butter, but you will need a 1kg/2lb lobster for 2 people. Thermidor was the eleventh month of the Revolutionary calendar in France, which in 1794, the year of the overthrow of Robespierre, ran from 19 July to 17 August. Lobster Thermidor is a dish of rich, intense flavours – what else could it be with such a name! – and you need just one 900g/2lb lobster for 4 people. Ask your fishmonger to prepare the lobster for you.

Remove all the flesh from the lobster shell, but leave the body and tail sections whole if you want to use them as serving dishes. Cut the meat into 1cm/½ inch dice. To make the Béchamel sauce, pour the milk into a non-stick saucepan and whisk in the flour until it is thoroughly blended. Add the butter and bring gently to the boil, whisking every minute or so. When it has fully thickened and is just bubbling, turn the heat right down and whisk thoroughly until you have a smooth, silky texture. Add the nutmeg and season with salt. The double cream or fromage frais will give it extra texture, but if you add fromage frais, don't boil the sauce again.

Stir the mustard into the Béchamel sauce, season generously, then stir in the lobster meat until it is well-coated in the sauce. Pile this mixture into the shells – or you can use a gratin dish, if you prefer – sprinkle with the Gruyère cheese, and put under a preheated grill for 4–5 minutes until the cheese has melted and the sauce is bubbling. Serve with saffron rice or mashed potatoes and plenty of crusty French bread, with a green salad to follow.

Petits Pois à la Française
PEAS COOKED IN THE FRENCH STYLE

Serves 4

½ lettuce heart or
1 Little Gem lettuce

6 spring onions

25g/1oz butter

450g/1lb shelled fresh or
frozen peas

120ml/4fl oz water

250ml/8fl oz
double cream (or single
cream if you feel guilty)

Salt and freshly ground
black pepper

This archetypal French dish is actually Italian! It was brought to France in the sixteenth century by the formidable Florentine heiress Catherine de' Medici, then the bride of the French King Henri II. With her she brought her own Italian cooks, who carried with them a vegetable wholly new to France – the green pea. They became the most *haut* of *haute cuisine* and anyone who was anyone feasted on green peas and bread!

Somewhat less majestically, Ogden Nash has a fine poem about the pea:

> I eat my peas with honey,
> I've done it all my life,
> It makes the peas taste funny,
> But it keeps them on the knife.

Shred the lettuce and spring onions into little ribbons with a sharp knife. Put the butter into a good solid pan with a lid – non-stick is best. Add the onions and lettuce and let them melt together. If the peas are fresh, add them at this point with the water and cook gently for about 10 minutes. If the peas are frozen, let the spring onions and lettuce cook on their own for 7–8 minutes, then add the frozen peas and cook for a further 2–3 minutes. Don't add the water, there is enough in the frozen peas already. Pour in the cream, balance the seasoning and bring to the boil, but don't let it cook for more than a minute more. The peas will be green, firm and surrounded in the most delicious and wicked sauce. Serve either with plain grilled meat or as a dish on its own in little bowls, with good bread.

Lobster Thermidor
(page 30)

Parfait Parisienne au Gingembre
PARISIAN GINGER ICECREAM

Serves 4

3 eggs

2 tablespoons icing sugar

2 tablespoons runny honey

250ml/8fl oz double cream

2 tablespoons finely chopped stem ginger

This is one of the nicest and easiest of puddings. The French have a huge taste for icecream and they make a lot of quite sophisticated and complex dishes with it. This is a smooth, creamy icecream to be eaten on its own and is very delicate and easy to make. It does contain raw eggs, so make sure you buy them from somewhere where you know they'll be salmonella-free; otherwise it may be advisable to avoid serving this to the very old, very young, the sick, or pregnant women.

You need 2 bowls for this and a whisk. In 1 bowl, whisk 1 whole egg and 2 egg yolks together until they thicken and turn creamy yellow. Whisk in the icing sugar, one tablespoon at a time, and then the runny honey. Whisk the whole thing until it is thick and foamy. In the other bowl, with a clean whisk, whisk the cream until it's absolutely rock hard. Add that to the egg mixture, folding it carefully so you don't knock out all the air. Stir in the chopped stem ginger. Pour the whole lot into a plastic container with a lid and put it in the freezer for at least 4 hours. It will last in there for a month. When you are ready to use it, take it out of the freezer and leave it to stand in the fridge for 1 hour before serving. It is smooth and creamy with the combined bite of the ginger and lusciousness of the honey.

PARISIAN CHEESEBOARD

Paris is a wonderful and exciting centre for food, and most of the truly great cheeses of France can be found there. But to my mind, for a cheeseboard that represents the best of Paris, there is only one choice, and that is Brie. It is available all over Britain, in varying forms, and it is well worth seeking out the best.

It is not of course produced in the centre of the city, but in the Île de France, just to the east of Paris. It is one of the great cheeses, mild, creamy and now made all over the cheese-eating world! It actually originated in the Île de France around 700 years ago, and that is where the best French Brie is still made.

The most famous is probably Brie de Meaux, followed by Brie de Melun, both of which are AOC cheeses, then Brie de Montereau and Brie de Coulommiers, which is sometimes called simply Coulommiers. They are made with both pasteurized and unpasteurized milk and the fat content of Brie can vary widely. Brie de Melun is sometimes sprinkled with powdered charcoal and is described as blue.

I think the ultimate Brie is the 60% unpasteurized, but it should be taken in small portions as it is very seriously rich and full of calories! Brie should be creamy all the way through. If it has a chalky bit in the middle, don't buy it, it isn't yet ripe. To end a large dinner party, I can't think of anything finer than a perfectly ripe wheel of Brie, still on its straw mat, accompanied simply by Muscat grapes.

Crème Renversée
CRÈME CARAMEL

Serves 4

300ml/10fl oz single cream

300ml/10fl oz milk

2 tablespoons vanilla sugar or 2 tablespoons caster sugar and a few drops vanilla essence

2 eggs

1 egg yolk

2 tablespoons granulated sugar

1 tablespoon water

Crème Caramel is one of the smoothest, creamiest, most delicious ways to end a meal.

Gently heat the cream and milk in a saucepan with the vanilla sugar or caster sugar and vanilla essence, until the sugar has dissolved. Be careful not to let it boil. Cool slightly, then beat the eggs and egg yolk and whisk them into the mixture. In a separate saucepan, dissolve the granulated sugar and water until it thickens and turns golden brown. Don't overboil. Pour this caramel into 4 small ramekins. Allow to cool, then strain the custard mixture on to the caramel through a sieve.

Place the ramekins in a *bain-marie* or roasting tin filled with water to come halfway up the ramekins, and bake in a low oven at 150°C/140°C fan/300°F/Gas Mark 2, or the bottom of the Aga, for 45–50 minutes. Take them out of the oven and leave to cool. To serve, loosen the edges of the crème with a palette knife, put a small plate over the top of each ramekin and turn it over. Give the base a sharp tap and the crème caramel should slide effortlessly out on to the plate, ready to eat.

THE MIDI

The name 'Midi' is a loose description, its literal meaning being the hot midday sun beating down on the South of France. More a realm of the imagination than of geography, this is the part of France also known as Langue d'Oc – the region where 'oc' was used for the word 'yes' rather than 'oui', which was the northern French form. Indeed, in parts of the South a strange sort of Languedoc nationalism is resurgent. The countryside in this area is relatively untouched as far as tourism is concerned, although in the last hundred years its economic situation has been transformed by the influx of holiday-makers rushing to the sunbelt. The Midi has always been a difficult part of the country, intellectually, religiously and physically. In the Middle Ages it was the centre of a devastating split from the Catholic Church known as the Albigensian Heresy. Centred around the town of Albi this split lasted nearly a hundred years and was only finally healed after much bloodshed. It cannot be entirely a coincidence that when another split occurred, some 250 years later, the Pope fled to another town in the area, Avignon. His palace, with its extraordinary bedroom, can still be seen there.

Geographically, the Midi is a strip of land that lies between Provence and the Atlantic. It enjoys a southern climate but is quite different in character: the people have a certain sturdy independence which is reflected in their cooking. Because the region borders Spain, the influence of the Basque people is strong – particularly where the coast turns down towards Barcelona and the Catalanspeaking area of Spain. Along the Mediterranean coast the ancient towns of Sète and Aigues-Mortes still maintain an air of almost medieval isolation on the edge of the great marsh district of the Camargue, with its famous flamingos, white bulls and gypsies. It is along this coastline, too, that alternatives to the inevitable *bouillabaisse* have really developed. Here, *bourride* dominates, based on the rich flavours of *aïoli*, the local garlic mayonnaise. In the Midi, the famous green herb butter used on grilled fish was first developed, with its mixture of sorrel, parsley and chives adding pungency as well as colour. There is still a major role for olive oil, olives, garlic and tomatoes which crop up all along the Mediterranean coast.

Inland, the food is unexpectedly substantial. Perhaps the most famous dish of all is *cassoulet*, a bean stew made with one of a wide

Opposite: The village of Estaing on the River Lot in the département of Aveyron.

variety of the dried beans given the generic name *haricots*. The other ingredients of this dish are a matter for serious dispute from town to town, with Toulouse, Castelnaudary and Carcassonne vying for premier place. The question of whether the meat that goes in with the beans should be mutton or pork, sausage or goose, is a matter of long-standing and probably everlasting dispute. What is beyond doubt is the deliciousness of the dish, particularly on a chilly autumn evening.

One of the most striking features of this region is the amount of turkey that is produced and eaten here. Escoffier, the nineteenth-century chef, mentions it in one of his notebooks, but historically it is not an ingredient usually associated with French cooking. More recently, however, portioned turkey pieces, including the enormous drumsticks for boning and stuffing, have become commonplace in butchers and supermarkets.

Another unexpected and fairly recent influence comes from the North African coast. A great number of *pieds noirs*, ex-French settlers from North Africa, came back to the Languedoc area and brought with them a taste for a variety of spicy dishes and condiments. This included couscous, which is seen in a surprising range of local restaurants. They also brought with them spicy lamb or lamb and chicken/turkey sausages called *merguez*, which are now commonplace throughout the area.

The vegetables and fruits are those you find all over the South, although in the Languedoc area in particular figs are widespread. Ripe figs eaten with delicious local honey and a bowlful of thick mild yoghurt is a breakfast to be savoured on a vine-covered terrace in the summer of the Midi.

If you are travelling in the area, honey and longer-lasting fruits such as the wonderful scented melons are worth buying on your way home – and so too is one of the greatest of all French cheeses, Roquefort, which is produced in limestone caves in the hills just below where the Massif Central rears up towards the centre of France. This blue/green-veined cheese is made from ewes' milk under strict *appellation contrôlée* conditions. In some of the specialist cheese shops in the towns nearest to Roquefort the most amazing selection of this cheese can be seen, all deserving the title but going up in rarity, quality and price to the precious green-veined special reserve cheese that is aged in the cave of the directors of the company and only rarely released to the public. The last time I found some it cost £10 per pound, but it was well worth it. However, unless you have a cool-bag system, don't try and travel with it – eat it as soon as you can with some of the superb local multigrain bread and some fresh grapes.

The Midi is not a great place for restaurants, and even Michelin has some surprising sweeps of blankness. Picnics seem to be the thing to have, and I would recommend rounding them off with one of the superb *tartes aux noix* or walnut tarts that are a speciality of many of the bakers and pâtisseries in the region. They are a kind of super-rich and very solid treacle tart, stuffed full of fresh local walnuts.

Salade de Tomates
TOMATO SALAD

This recipe is simple and hugely typical of the region. You'd be hard pushed to find a restaurant or a home in the Midi which doesn't serve this at least once a day. It is especially good in the summer, when those great big red juicy tomatoes that seem to taste of the sun are available. You can also make this very successfully with baby or cherry tomatoes which have a lovely sweet flavour. The type of onion is also important. Don't use a strong English onion, the kind that makes your eyes water; buy a salad variety. You can find either white or purple ones.

Wash the tomatoes and if they're big ones, slice them thickly. If they're baby tomatoes, just cut them in half. Arrange them in over-lapping layers in an attractive dish. Break up the onion slices and sprinkle them over the tomatoes. You can snip the basil with scissors, which is the traditional way – and sprinkle that over the salad. Put the red wine vinegar, salt and French mustard into a bowl and whisk until well blended, or put them into a jar with a screw-top lid and shake it very well. Add the olive oil and either whisk or shake again until thoroughly blended, then pour the dressing immediately over the salad. You can serve it at once, but this salad improves hugely by being left for a little while, though no more than 30 minutes. Unlike green salads, it doesn't wilt and the flavours blend and develop. Serve with crusty French bread – that's essential!

Serves 4

450g/1lb ripe sweet tomatoes

1 mild onion, peeled and thinly sliced

1 tablespoon finely chopped fresh basil

For the dressing:

1 tablespoon red wine vinegar

½ teaspoon salt

½ teaspoon made French mustard

4 tablespoons olive oil

Piperade (page 47)
Steak Vignerons
(page 46)

Soupe de Poivrons aux Tomates
RED PEPPER AND TOMATO SOUP

Serves 4

450g/1lb ripe tomatoes

2 large red peppers

1 bunch spring onions

4 tablespoons olive oil

Salt and freshly ground black pepper

900ml/1½ pints vegetable or chicken stock

1 teaspoon caster sugar

4 tablespoons low-fat fromage frais

Tomatoes ripened in the sun of the Midi have a marvellous intensity of flavour. Even if we don't have the luxury here of picking a warm tomato off the vine, if you buy the best tomatoes available this soup will have a rich, clear taste and vivid colour.

Cut the tomatoes in half and scoop out the watery bits. Cut the red peppers in half and scoop out the seeds and all the white bits. Cut the tomatoes and peppers into 1 cm/½ inch pieces and keep a few pieces of pepper on one side for decoration. Trim the spring onions and cut the white part only into 1 cm/½ inch pieces. Keep the green bits.

Heat the olive oil in a large pan and fry the vegetables gently for 5 minutes, then season generously. Add the stock, bring to the boil and simmer for 10 minutes. Pour the soup into a food processor or liquidizer – you will probably have to do it in 2 lots. Add the green part of the spring onions and the sugar and whizz until it's smooth. Serve in individual bowls with a piece of pepper floating on the top, and spoon some of the fromage frais on to each piece of pepper.

Bourride
FISH SOUP WITH GARLIC MAYONNAISE

Serves 4

700g/1½lb fillets of monkfish, haddock or bream, preferably skinned

4 thick slices white bread, toasted

For the *court bouillon*:

1 onion, peeled and halved

½ lemon

1 bay leaf

6 peppercorns

1 teaspoon salt

1.2 litre/2 pints water

Bourride is the second of the two great traditional fish soups from the South of France. One is bouillabaisse, which comes from Nice and Cannes and along that bit of the coast (see p. 168). The other is bourride, which you find more often here in South-West France. It's a very attractive, easy-to-make dish, with three separate stages to it. It is based on aïoli, the garlic-flavoured mayonnaise, and also uses rouille (see p. 16), which is aïoli with a few drops of chilli sauce. If you don't want to make your own, you can buy both aïoli and rouille in most big supermarkets or speciality shops.

Into a large saucepan put the ingredients for the *court bouillon* – the onion, lemon, bay leaf, peppercorns, salt and water. Bring to the boil and let it simmer for 20 minutes. Take out the lemon and add the fish. Simmer for about 10 minutes until the fish is just cooked but not falling apart. Take the fish out of the water and keep it warm. Put each slice of toast in a soup bowl and moisten with a tablespoon of the fish stock. Lay the fish in equal portions on top.

In a separate saucepan, take half the aïoli, which is approximately a cupful, a cup of stock and the cornflour. Mix them together thoroughly and bring gently to the boil so the sauce just thickens. Pour this over the fish. Mix another 2–3 tablespoons of the aïoli with the chilli sauce and serve that separately as rouille to eat with the fish. Serve on its own, with a salad or vegetables afterwards. This dish is served warm, not hot.

For the sauces:

1 measure aïoli (p.16)

1 teaspoon cornflour

1 teaspoon chilli sauce

Cuisse de Dinde Midi
TURKEY LEGS WITH HERB STUFFING AU MIDI

Until recently, the French were not great turkey eaters, not even at Christmas. But suddenly all over France, and particularly down in the South-West, turkey pieces have become available in supermarkets and on restaurant menus. Either the French have bought shares in a turkey farm, or they've discovered, as we have, that it is a delicious and low-fat alternative to veal. This is an ideal dish for low-fat cooking, especially if you use fromage frais rather than crème fraîche. Turkey thighs are about the size of large chicken thighs, and because they are sold boneless you can stuff them. Herbs are a great feature of cooking in the southern regions of France, and if you happen to have any lavender in your garden, you can put it to good use here.

Make the stuffing first. Put the slice of bread, the spring onions, the herbs and the egg into a food processor. Whizz everything until it's chopped and blended together. Divide the mixture into 8, and carefully stuff the boned thighs – don't cram it in – roll them closed and secure each with a cocktail stick. Remember to remove the cocktail stick before serving! Heat the olive oil in a pan large enough to hold all the turkey thighs and sauté them gently for about 15 minutes. Turn them so they brown completely. Wash and trim the button mushrooms. Cut them in half and add them to the pan with the chicken stock. Bring to the boil, then simmer for another 5–10 minutes until the thighs are completely cooked.

Take the turkey and mushrooms out of the pan and keep warm. Spoon in the crème fraîche or fromage frais and stir well. If you are using crème fraîche you can boil it, otherwise just heat the fromage frais through – don't allow it to boil or it will separate. When the sauce has thickened and turned creamy, pour it over the turkey and mushrooms. Season generously and serve with new potatoes and either green beans or mangetout.

Serves 4

8 boneless turkey thighs

2 tablespoons olive oil

100g/4oz button mushrooms

120ml/4fl oz chicken stock

4 tablespoons crème fraîche or fromage frais

For the stuffing:

1 slice white bread

4 spring onions, trimmed

Pinch each of fresh rosemary and thyme

Pinch of lavender (optional)

1 egg

Walnut Tart
(page 49)

Entrecôtes Vignerons
STEAK VIGNERONS

Serves 4

4 entrecôte steaks, about 175g/6oz each

1 tablespoon each oil and butter

100g/4oz shallots or 1 small onion, peeled and finely chopped

4 tablespoons red wine vinegar

250ml/8fl oz beef stock or water

Salt and freshly ground black pepper

A good handful finely chopped fresh parsley

This recipe originated in the wine-growing areas of France, though you can now find it all over the place. Like so many other dishes, it has undergone certain refinements and it is increasingly common to find that the wine used in the deglazing process has been replaced by fine vinegars or vinegars of varying flavours, like balsamic vinegar or vinegars flavoured with sherry or raspberries, and that's the technique used here. This dish also needs shallots, which are the same colour as onions but have the shape of a large clove of garlic. The taste is milder than an onion and very distinctive. They are well worth buying in season. If you can't find them, a small onion will do.

Trim the fat and any gristle off the steaks, or alternatively you can slash them to stop them curling. In a frying pan large enough to take all the steaks, heat the oil and butter together. Brown the steaks rapidly for 1½–2 minutes on 1 side, then turn them over and cook for the same amount of time on the other side, if you like them rare. If you prefer your steak medium rather than rare, cook for 2½ minutes each side, and if you like them ruined, leave them there for 3–3½ minutes each side. When you turn the steaks over, add the peeled and finely chopped shallots (or onion).

When the steaks are cooked, put them on to hot plates but leave the shallots in the pan. Deglaze the pan with the red wine vinegar. Stir it round so the vinegar picks up all the lovely crusty bits stuck to the bottom of the pan. When the vinegar is really bubbling, add the stock or water. Stir it all together, bring back to the boil and allow it to reduce for just 1 minute until it becomes quite syrupy. Pour that over the steaks, season with salt and pepper and sprinkle very generously with the chopped parsley. Serve with new potatoes, or even sauté or roast potatoes.

Piperade
PIPERADE

Piperade is as popular in south-west France as it is over the border in the Basque country of Spain. It is often described as an omelette, but it isn't really; it is much more a grand scrambled egg with a rich stew of tomatoes and sweet peppers. You can add meat or fish to it, but I prefer this basic, simple recipe. It is wonderful served hot with warm French bread, though in France they often serve it cold as an hors d'oeuvre.

Heat the oil in a large non-stick pan and fry the peppers and onions gently for 5–7 minutes until softened but not browned. Halve the tomatoes, scoop out and throw away any seeds and slice the tomatoes thinly. Put them into the pan with the chopped garlic and the butter. Break the eggs into a bowl and beat them until they are mixed but not frothy. Season the vegetables generously and add the eggs to the tomato, pepper and onion mixture, scrambling them continuously over a medium heat until they are creamy but not set hard. Add the lemon juice, stir one last time and serve before the eggs become too firm.

Serves 4

2 tablespoons oil

2 large red peppers, de-seeded and thinly sliced

1 large green pepper, de-seeded and thinly sliced

225g/8oz Spanish onions, thinly sliced

225g/8oz large, ripe tomatoes

1 clove garlic, peeled and finely chopped

25g/1oz butter

6 eggs

Salt and freshly ground black pepper

Juice of ½ lemon

Haricots d'Espagne Midi
RUNNER BEANS MIDI

Runner beans on their own are delicious, but cooking them with tomatoes and garlic turns them into a splendid dish. You can eat it by itself, but it also goes very well with grilled fish or meat.

Trim and string the beans and wash them, then cut them into thin strips. Heat the oil in a shallow sauté pan or frying pan with a lid. Put the beans in and turn them for about 1½ minutes. Add the chopped garlic to the pan, stir, and leave for another minute or so; together the beans should fry gently for about three minutes. Add a cup of water – just enough so the beans are swimming a bit. Turn the heat up and let them cook until the water has nearly gone.

Meanwhile, halve the tomatoes, and if they are full of runny seeds scoop some of them out so you are left with the flesh. Chop the tomatoes finely. Just before all the water in the pan has gone, add the tomatoes, salt and pepper and stir for just 2 minutes. The whole cooking time should not be longer than about 8 minutes, so the beans are still crisp and bright green, but now flavoured with the garlic, the olive oil and the slight sweetness of tomatoes. Serve them immediately.

Serves 2–4

450g/1lb runner beans

2 tablespoons olive oil

1 clove garlic, peeled and finely chopped

2 large ripe tomatoes

Salt and freshly ground black pepper

Épinards à l'Ail
SPINACH WITH GARLIC

Serves 4

450g/1lb pack ready-prepared fresh spinach

½ clove garlic

1 tablespoon olive oil

1 tablespoon butter

Spinach is such a delight to cook these days as it comes ready prepared and washed. On its own it is marvellously fresh and delicious, but this slight touch of garlic works very well. Whatever you do, don't overcook it!

Rinse the spinach once more and add to a large pan of boiling water which you have salted generously. Allow to cook for just 2 minutes, then drain very thoroughly. Rub a frying pan with the cut side of the half clove of garlic. Heat the oil in the pan, then add the butter. When the butter has thoroughly melted, swirl the oil and butter mixture round the pan, add the spinach, and turn it for 2 minutes until it is thoroughly coated and glistening with the lovely buttery, garlicky juices. Serve immediately. This goes well with fish or meat, and I have been known to eat it as a dish on its own.

MIDI CHEESEBOARD

Sheep and goats roam the warm rocky pastures of the Auvergne and Languedoc, producing milk which makes some of the most splendid cheeses in France. The best of them travel well, and are available in supermarkets here: Saint Nectaire, Bleu d'Auvergne, Saint Augur, and the noblest of them all, the great Roquefort. The 4 together make a well-balanced and delicious cheeseboard,

though there are others well worth trying.

Roquefort comes from a small village in Aveyron. It is one of the oldest known cheeses, smooth, creamy and blue-veined. It is made from ewes' milk and has a strong, rich flavour and smell. The milk can be brought in from Corsica and a few other places, but the true Roquefort has to be matured in the natural limestone caves of the

mountains of Cambelou. It is wonderful just to eat, but it is also great in cooking.

Other blue-veined cheeses to include in your Midi cheeseboard are Bleu d'Auvergne, firm with a strong flavour, and Saint Augur, a rich blue-veined cheese, with a soft tang to it.

Cantal is also worth seeking out, though you will probably have to buy it in a specialist shop here.

It is a firm cows' milk cheese, with a sweet, nutty flavour that intensifies as the cheese ripens. It also cooks very well (see Gougère, p. 106). It is a huge cheese – cylindrical in shape, about 35–40cm/14–16 inches high, and it weighs 30–45kg/75–100lb. Its flavour contrasts well with the blue cheeses, as does Saint Nectaire, an ancient cheese with a marvellous earthy flavour and smell.

Tarte aux Noix
WALNUT TART

This is a wonderfully rich tart – a great speciality of the Midi region around Carcassonne which is famous for it. As you might imagine, walnuts grow all over this region. Tarte aux Noix also uses honey, which is another major product from this area.

To bake a pastry case blind, roll out the pâte sablée and use it to line a flan dish. Prick it all over and bake it in a hot oven at 200°C/180°C fan/400°F/Gas Mark 6, or the middle of an Aga roasting oven, for about 10 minutes. Take it out of the oven. Crush the walnuts until they're in bits about the size of half a peanut. The easiest way is to put the shelled walnuts into a bag and crush them with a rolling pin. Whisk the eggs and mix in the crushed walnuts, the honey and the cream until they are thoroughly amalgamated. Add the nutmeg and cinnamon, stir and pour the whole mixture into the pastry case.

Bake it in a medium oven at 180°C/160°C fan/350°F/Gas Mark 4, or the bottom of an Aga roasting oven, for about 30 minutes, until the mixture is bubbling and slightly risen. Take it out of the oven and allow it to cool – it sinks a bit as this happens but don't worry about it. This is, by the way, not a tart to eat hot. When it's cool, sprinkle the top with a thin layer of icing sugar for decoration. It looks marvellous, with the dark rich gold of the filling breaking through the whiteness of the icing sugar. Cut it into quite thin slices: this is seriously rich!

Serves 4

1 pastry case, baked blind from the pâte sablée (French sweet pastry recipe, see below), or there are very good ones you can buy

350g/12oz walnuts

3 eggs

4 tablespoons honey

2 tablespoons double cream

Pinch each nutmeg and cinnamon

1–2 teaspoons icing sugar

HOW TO MAKE PÂTE SABLÉE (FRENCH SWEET PASTRY)

Pâte sablée is the French sweet pastry that is so delicious that you can roll out the bits left over and make biscuits from them. It is a crumblier and sweeter pastry than our shortcrust – it melts in the mouth – and is easier to roll out thinly. It doesn't take long to make, especially in a food processor.

Method:
You can make the pastry either by hand or in a food processor. Put the flour, butter, sugar and salt into the processor and whizz until the mixture resembles fine breadcrumbs. Add the egg yolk and process again, then add the water. I use half an egg-shell at a time, until suddenly the pastry binds together and makes a ball around the blade of the processor. At that moment, stop. If you're making it by hand, knead it until you feel it beginning to give, and instead of being hard and lumpy, becoming pliable. You may need a little less water than if you are using a food processor. Whichever way you have made it, pat it into a sort of ball and press it firmly with the heel of your hand. This pushes the air out and makes the pastry ready to relax. Wrap it in clingfilm and leave it to rest for 30 minutes in the fridge before using. If you don't leave it for that 30 minutes, it will shrink when you cook it.

How to use it:
Pâte sablée is the pastry to use for most fruit and other sweet tarts – see Tarte aux Noix above.

100g/4oz plain flour

65g/2½oz butter

50g/2oz cup caster sugar

½ teaspoon salt

1 egg yolk

1–2 tablespoons cold water

LYON

Lyon is the second city of France. There are one or two places that would dispute this title, but there is no question that the great southern centre where the Saône and the Rhône come together is the counterbalance to Paris – and if the Lyonnais are to be believed it is certainly the pre-eminent city in France for food. This is not a reputation based on delicacy, although the quality of cooking is extremely high. The Lyonnais love onions with everything, eat salad with most meals, and consume the most amazing quantities of offal – in particular tripe. They also eat sausages, chickens and almost anything that grows or moves. The exception to this is fish, which is not common except for *quenelles de brochet* or pike dumplings. The *quenelles* are delicious if you can find ones that have been well made. Unfortunately the majority tend to be factory-produced and lacking in the delicate, almost soufflé-like lightness that has made the dish so famous. In the many bistros and working men's restaurants throughout the city a more substantial bill of fare is still to be found.

The great reputation of Lyon's restaurants was made at the beginning of this century by a series of female restaurateurs – a phenomenon unusual in France. Mère Fillioux and her successor Mère Brazier were the queens of a movement which established a set menu at lunchtime that might include truffle chicken, the above-mentioned *quenelles*, artichoke hearts stuffed with *foie gras*, as well as hors d'oeuvre, cheese and a famous praline icecream for dessert – cooking for serious trenchermen!

Food is certainly my lasting impression of Lyon, which I first visited one evening a third of a century ago, when the great September fair was in full swing. Fresh from the ration coupons of England, I was most struck by the first course in a tiny back-street restaurant: a pyramid of mushrooms cooked in a mixture of oil and butter, flavoured with garlic and parsley. The dish towered to such a height that even six of us – two of us had never seen so many mushrooms in our lives before – could not finish it. Those mushrooms live on in my memory as one of the finest examples of generosity and abundance in French cooking. In addition to their enthusiasm for

Opposite: The River Saône in Lyon.

meat and mushrooms, the Lyonnais have an enormous taste for pumpkin, which they eat in both savoury and sweet forms. They also enjoy hearty soups and rich puddings, which is startling when you consider the amount of food that has gone before.

If you are visiting the region, perhaps on your way south towards the sea, and turn off the clearly signed motorway routes, beware! Lyon is one of the most difficult cities to find your way around – not least because of the complexity of bridges created by the confluence of the two great rivers. It is also very difficult, for some reason, to find your way through Lyon when travelling north on the motorway, and I have always managed to grind to a halt over that particular trip. In spite of this, a stop in Lyon can be extraordinarily rewarding: the inhabitants' hospitality is legendary, and their pride in their own culinary traditions so palpable that a request for advice on somewhere to eat will almost certainly produce a detailed, involved argument among your advisers, more often than not followed by an invitation to join them.

Lyon is not really a tourist city but a great industrial centre and an inland port, the Rhône still being a major highway through France. It is also one of the country's major financial centres and a great university city. It doesn't offer the sort of portable specialities that tourists might choose to take back with them – there is no central Lyon cheese, for example, although to the west of the city the highlands of the Auvergne do supply Cantal, a hard cheese not unlike Cheddar, and two famous blue cheeses, Bleu d'Auvergne and Fourme d'Anbert, which are second only to Roquefort in French estimation. The best memento of Lyon would be to eat with the locals and take away the warm memories that their generosity, love of life and substantial cuisine provide.

Oeufs Surprise
SURPRISE EGGS

If you were to eat this amazing dish in a 3-star restaurant in Lyon, the caviare would be Beluga and the bill would suggest you had just won the lottery! You can, however, make a very passable copy of the 3-star version, using either cheaper sturgeon caviare, which is still very expensive, or go for a different fish roe altogether. Lumpfish roe is the cheapest, then trout, and next come the beautiful deep pink salmon eggs, which are my favourite. The surprise with these eggs is the presentation. If you have pretty eggcups, the dish looks even more stunning.

You need a very sharp knife and a little bit of nerve for this. Cut the tops off the egg shells at the pointed end, leaving a lid of about 1cm/½ inch high in each case. If you do this timidly, the shell is likely to crack untidily rather than slice off neatly. Be bold! Tip the eggs into a bowl, and rinse and lightly dry the empty egg shells. Put these ready in the eggcups.

Five minutes before you are ready to eat, lightly beat the eggs, and heat the butter with the lemon juice in a saucepan. Add the eggs and scramble them quickly until they are cooked but still slightly soft. Pile the eggs into the shells, leaving a little space at the top. You may have some scrambled egg left over. Put 2 teaspoons of soured cream on top of each egg and then a teaspoon of your chosen caviare on top of that. Cover the lot with the reserved shell lid and serve immediately with elegantly thin, hot buttered toast.

Serves 4

4 large free-range eggs

50g/2oz butter

Juice of ½ lemon

50ml/2fl oz soured cream

1 pot of caviare – sturgeon, salmon or lumpfish – about 25g/1oz

Pâté de Foie de Volaille
CHICKEN LIVER PÂTÉ

Chicken livers make marvellous rich, smooth pâtés. This one is light and elegant enough for a dinner party. Serve it with little green gherkins called *cornichons*.

Wash the livers well. Melt three-quarters of the butter in a non-stick frying pan. Add the livers and garlic and sauté over a high heat for 3–4 minutes until the livers are brown on the outside but still just a little bit pink in the centre. Tip the contents of the frying pan into a food processor or liquidizer, add the herbs and apple juice and process until smooth. Season generously and tip into a soufflé dish or pretty serving dish. Smooth the top carefully. Melt the remaining butter in the saucepan and pour through a sieve (to catch the white bits) over the top of the pâté. Chill for at least 6 hours before eating. It will keep in the fridge for up to 5 days.

Serves 4

225g/8oz chicken livers

100g/4oz butter

1 clove garlic, peeled and finely chopped

1 teaspoon freeze-dried or chopped fresh thyme

1 teaspoon freeze-dried or chopped fresh oregano

1 wine glass apple juice

Salt and freshly ground black pepper

Potage de Potiron
PUMPKIN SOUP

Serves 4

450g/1lb pumpkin in its shell

900ml/1½ pints chicken stock, home-made, frozen or a very good stock cube

2 sprigs fresh parsley, stalks separated and leaves chopped

225g/8oz tomatoes

Salt and freshly ground black pepper

One of the wonderful things about the Lyonnais region is the great range of cooking styles. While today Lyon and its surroundings are home to some of the greatest modern chefs in France, the tradition of hearty cooking goes back over the centuries. This pumpkin soup is warm and filling, with a delicate and delicious flavour.

Peel the pumpkin from its shell and clear away any soft woolly bits with seeds on. You should be left with about 350g/12oz of bright, firm golden pumpkin. Cut the flesh into 1cm/½ inch dice. In a large saucepan, bring the chicken stock to the boil, add the pumpkin and parsley stalks and simmer for 15–18 minutes until the pumpkin is tender. Don't cook it too long or it will turn into mush. Cut the tomatoes into 1cm/½ inch pieces, and add to the soup. Season generously and simmer for another 5 minutes until the tomatoes and pumpkins are both cooked. Stir in the finely chopped parsley leaves and that's it – this is not a soup you blend. It is meant to have fine little pieces of vegetables which give the most marvellous colour contrast – the dark red of the tomatoes, the orange of the pumpkin and the bright green of the parsley in a golden liquid. The flavour is delicate and super!

HOW TO MAKE AN OMELETTE

3 eggs, preferably free-range as the flavour of the egg matters hugely

A walnut-sized piece of butter

Salt and freshly ground black pepper

The great secret of a good French omelette is that it is not a pancake but rather a plump cushion. Although it appears to be very easy to make, properly cooked it constitutes part of French *haute cuisine*. One of the key people in this was a famous French restaurateuse called Mère Brazier, whose restaurant was in the hills above Lyon. The ingredients may be straightforward, but the trick is all in the technique and the pan you use. In fact, you always need a smaller pan than you think you do. For a 3-egg omelette, you only need a 12cm/5 inch frying pan, and that is really quite small. If you're a man, the spread of your hand is about 23cm/9 inches, and if you're a woman, the spread of your hand is about 19cm/7½ inches, so you need a pan that is smaller than the spread of your hand by a lot! For a 6-egg omelette, use a 25cm/10 inch pan, but I think they are better made individually.

Method:
The pan needs to be either non-stick or very well greased. In a bowl lightly beat the 3 eggs. Heat the butter in the pan until it foams and hisses. The moment it stops hissing pour in the eggs and, with the back of a fork, stir them gently in the hot butter for about a minute, drawing the edges to the middle until all the egg is cooked. Season generously. While the middle is still a little moist, fold it with a palette knife or a fork and tip it on to a warm plate. The omelette will go on cooking for another 35 seconds to a minute after you have taken it out, so unless you like eggy shoe leather, take it out of the pan just before it is cooked, and serve at once.

Champignons Lyonnaise
BUTTERED HERBED MUSHROOMS

Serves 4

700g/1½lb chestnut or button mushrooms

75g/3oz butter

½ clove garlic, peeled and finely chopped

2 tablespoons each chopped fresh parsley and chopped fresh chives

Salt and freshly ground black pepper

This is simply one of the best dishes I've ever eaten. I first came across it when I visited Lyon as a teenager. I was taken out to a dinner which went on for 5 or 6 courses and, while I can remember all of it vividly, it is the mushrooms which stand out, a great buttery, herbed pile of them. They were served as a separate course *after* the meat. Coming from what was still rationed Britain after the war, I had never seen food so abundantly served! For this recipe I would strongly suggest chestnut mushrooms – dark brown, organically grown, with a real and substantial flavour.

Trim the mushrooms with a sharp knife, but do not peel them. Put them in a colander and pour over them a kettleful of boiling water. This sterilizes them, but leaves the flavour intact. Shake them dry. If the mushrooms are big, cut them in halves or quarters, otherwise leave them as they are. Heat the butter in a large pan, put in the garlic and soften it gently for a couple of minutes. Add the mushrooms, turn them in the butter, and put the lid on and cook for not more than 1½ minutes on maximum heat. The mushrooms steam, but do not become gloppy. They should be crisp and hot and garlicky. Sprinkle on the parsley and chives. Pile the mushrooms on each person's plate and then, and only then, season them with salt and black pepper. Eat them with lots of bread to soak up all those wonderful juices!

Carré d'Agneau Lyonnaise
RACK OF LAMB LYONNAIS

Serves 4

2 × 8-chop racks of lamb, trimmed and skinned

25g/1oz finely chopped parsley

1 teaspoon freeze-dried rosemary

3 tablespoons fine white fresh breadcrumbs

Grated rind of 1 lemon

1 egg, beaten

Rack of lamb is eaten all over France, but the lamb which comes from the huge plateau to the south of Lyon is particularly good. Each rack holds about 8 chops, so for 4 people you need to buy 2 racks. Your butcher may call it best end of neck. If you are buying from a butcher, ask him to chine the racks so that the chops can be easily separated with a carving knife when they are cooked.

Mix the parsley, rosemary, breadcrumbs and grated lemon rind together. Brush the skin side of the racks of lamb with the beaten egg and then press on the herb and breadcrumb mixture to form a coating – a sort of external stuffing. Put the racks together as if you were putting your fingers together in prayer so the bones interlock. It's what is known here as a 'guard of honour'.

Heat the oven to 200°C/180°C fan/400°F/Gas Mark 6, or use the top of an Aga roasting oven, and roast for 25 minutes. This will leave the meat a little pink. If you prefer your lamb well done, cook for a further 5–10 minutes. The breadcrumbs will be crisp and brown, and the meat tender and moist. Allow the lamb to stand for 5 minutes before carving. To serve, cut down between the chops so each person gets 4 chops arranged in a neat little fan on the plate. It is delicious with a little redcurrant jelly (though you won't find that in Lyon!), some new potatoes, lightly buttered, and a green vegetable such as spinach or mangetout.

Poulet Sauté à la Crème aux Ciboulettes
SAUTÉED CHICKEN WITH CREAM AND CHIVES

Some of the best chickens in France come from round Lyon – to the east, for example, is Bresse, where chickens with a marvellous, rich flavour are bred. There are countless chicken recipes from this area. Chicken with cream and chives is one of the simplest, quickest and most delicious. Although they are expensive, if you can find free-range chicken breasts, do use them. The flavour and texture are very good.

In a large frying pan heat the oil and butter. As soon as the sizzling stops, add the chicken breasts, skin side down, and sauté for 5 minutes until golden. Turn them over and sauté for another 10–15 minutes over a low heat. You may wish to put the lid on to help the chicken cook thoroughly.

When the chicken is cooked through, season generously and pour the cream on top of the chicken. Stir so all the bits in the pan are absorbed into the sauce, and allow the cream to come briefly to the boil. Take the chicken breasts out, and put them on to warmed plates. Add the chopped chives to the pan, stir well and pour the sauce over the chicken. Serve immediately.

Serves 4

1 tablespoon sunflower oil

1 tablespoon butter

4 boned chicken breasts, preferably free-range

Salt and freshly ground black pepper

150ml/5fl oz double cream

2 tablespoons chopped fresh chives

Mousse au Chocolat à l'Orange
CHOCOLATE AND ORANGE MOUSSE

Serves 4

Juice and grated rind of 1 orange

100g/4oz bitter dark chocolate

50g/2oz butter, preferably unsalted

4 large eggs, separated

Chocolate mousse seems to appear in one form or another on most French restaurant menus, though it is probably at its most sublime in the gastronomic temples round Lyon. This version has the smoothness of pure cream but tastes splendidly of chocolate, balanced brilliantly by the zest of citrus. Buy the bitterest chocolate you can find, preferably containing over 50% cocoa solids.

Put the orange juice into a heavy-based saucepan, add the broken-up chocolate and melt gently over a low heat, stirring constantly. When smooth, add the butter and grated orange rind, stirring until the butter melts, then beat the mixture until thick. Take the pan off the heat, stir in the egg yolks and heat briefly (unless you like chocolate scrambled eggs!) until the mixture is thick again. Leave to cool. Beat the egg whites until stiff, and fold into the cooled chocolate mixture. Pour into wine glasses and chill for at least 2 hours.

LYON CHEESEBOARD

Lyon is such a centre of marvellous gastronomy that it is hardly surprising that there are many fine cheeses from there and from the regions with rich pastureland which surround it. Cheeses from this area are made from ewes', goats' and cows' milk.

The best-known cheese is Bleu de Bresse, which is readily available. It is quite a modern cheese, smooth and creamy with blue veins running through it and a strong flavour.

Mont d'Or, one of the most famous of Lyonnais cheeses, can be bought here in specialist shops. Once made from goats' milk, or a mixture of goats' and cows' milk, these days it is generally made from cows' milk only. It is a lovely soft cheese with a delicate flavour and contrasts well with Bleu de Bresse.

Rigotte, which is made in a number of regions, is a cylindrical cheese with a pale gold-coloured rind that sometimes has a reddish blush. The creamy white cheese is firm, with a good, distinctive flavour, and can be made from goats' and cows' milk mixed, or just cows' milk. Rigotte in oil is the one to look out for here.

If you find yourself in Lyon itself, try one of the great traditions of the city – Cervelle de Canut. It is a soft curd cheese which is served in bars as a sort of sophisticated elevenses, seasoned and blended with shallots, herbs, cream, white wine and a little oil.

Poires Étuvées au Miel
PEARS BAKED WITH HONEY

Fruit from th:~
excep
Confer·
pudd;·

especially good, and its pears are no
ieed pears that aren't too ripe.
oo are Comice. This is a lovely, spicy
brown sauce.

Core the pears, leaving the stalks
k a clove in each pear and lay the
of dish. Scatter the cardamom seeds
n. To make the honey syrup, dis-
oiling water. Pour this over the
l by the liquid.
C/180°C fan/400°F/Gas Mark 6, or
for about 1 hour until they're ten-
vith cream, or let them go cold,
ner party, serve each pear in an
noney-flavoured sauce forming a

Serves 6

6 firm pears

6 cloves

8 cardamom seeds, cracked

2 cinnamon sticks

For the honey syrup:

2 tablespoons caster sugar

4–6 tablespoons clear honey

300–450ml/10–15fl oz cups boiling water

NORMANDY

Normandy is the French province which is perhaps closest to the heart of Britain. It is not the closest geographically, but ever since its bastard duke conquered the Anglo-Saxon kings of Wessex, Normandy and Britain have been closely linked; indeed, the Queen still retains the ancient title of Duke of Normandy. The region was originally settled by Vikings in the ninth century – the Nor Men who arrived at about the time that their Danish cousins were arriving on the east coast of Britain. Then, as now, Normandy was rich agricultural land and the raiders soon settled down to an ordered existence. Their descendants still have the bulk and size and slightly slower approach to life that sets them apart from their Celtic and Gallic neighbours. The region itself runs through the rich farming heartland of France, from the outskirts of Paris west along the banks of the Seine to the Atlantic at Honfleur. This is cattle and sheep country, rich with cream and spiced with Calvados, the region's famous apple brandy.

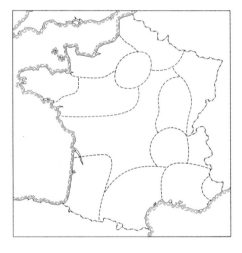

Normandy was fought over by the British and the French right up to the end of the reign of King John, and one of its great monuments, Château Gaillard, was built by John's elder brother, Richard Coeur de Lion. This beautiful castle was built high on a loop of the Seine to guard against – fruitlessly as it turned out – the incursions of the French. It is still worth visiting now, not least because you will also be visiting places you will think you have seen before. For this is the part of France where the Impressionist school of painters, led by Claude Monet, were based. On a spring morning you may, if you are lucky, come across an image of the Seine wreathed in mists, with the willows breaking green above them, and see in reality those images that have filled our minds for over a hundred years. If you visit Monet's house at Giverny, now a museum, you will discover that he wasn't just in love with painting but also with food – a serious and substantial pastime in Normandy. In his kitchen/dining room the table and chairs and plates and forks are still laid out as they were when he gave his famous luncheons and dinners, based on the extraordinary range of local products.

Normandy is in many ways to Paris what Kent is to London – its

Opposite: The beautiful
harbour at Honfleur.

kitchen garden. The region is blessed with a huge range of food. The coast provides some of the best North Atlantic fish and shellfish. It is cooked magnificently in the homes and quayside restaurants of the fishing towns that lie close to Mont-Saint Michel, which marks the border with Brittany. Although on the way south, Normandy often has cold and wet winters, and sometimes early autumns and late springs too. In the summer it becomes warm, but still retains the sort of greenness we associate with Britain or Ireland. At its best, along the banks of the Seine in high summer, it is perfect picnicking country – the ultimate place to eat crusty bread, fresh cheese and ripe fruit in the most golden sunlit meadows imaginable. Normandy is not wine country, although it is served in restaurants and homes. Cider is the real drink here, or perry, the pear equivalent. The marvellous cloudy, freshly pressed apple or pear juice is served before it has fermented and tastes delicious.

The Seine itself provides a huge range of freshwater fish, and the surrounding countryside offers beef and milk, cream and cheese, apples and pears with all their by-products, honey from the hives, and an amazingly rich range of vegetables grown in the region's fertile soil. This abundance of old-fashioned fruit and vegetables is turned into delicious old-fashioned dishes: salads of beetroot; beans cooked with garlic and butter; pancakes filled with grated apple; and pears baked in pastry and honey. This is not light eating: shellfish, pâtés and fish in cream sauces: game and duck cooked in local cider and cream – all rounded off with a glass of *trou normand*, literally 'norman hole', a fiery calvados regarded as an essential digestive to the rich food that has preceded it. Following this comes the extraordinary range of Normandy cheeses, featuring at least one of the celebrated local Camemberts, with fruit tarts and puddings to follow.

If the countryside, centred around France's great northern river, is beautiful, so too are the towns and cities of Normandy. Rouen, still largely medieval at its centre, has a small but extremely tall cathedral, and an ancient square where the spot where Joan of Arc was burned is marked by a spectacularly high-tech stainless-steel memorial. Next to this is an equally modern covered market where traditional foods are on sale: stalls selling cheeses and sausages, charcuterie and vegetables, fruit and preserves, are packed in together under the spare arches. Around the edge of the square medieval stone buildings house pastry and baker's shops where you will become aware of the other great passion of Normandy – sweet pastries and cakes. Fruit tarts are a speciality, with a layer of succulent *crème pâtissière* between the pastry and the fruit which is then glazed to a glistening perfection.

Honfleur is another architecturally fascinating town, with its sixteenth-century *bassin*, or inner port, still surrounded by tall granite traders' houses. Behind these lies a little square which contains the most extraordinary fishermen's church which looks as if it has been made out of two gigantic upturned wooden boats. Here, the emphasis is on fish, with a market on most mornings and restaurants selling local specialities. Look out in particular for dressed crabs and the French equivalent of whitebait, *friture*, a mixture of the small fish that fishermen used to eat themselves because they couldn't sell them and which now, like *bouillabaisse*, has become a highly fashionable dish.

Shopping for edible souvenirs is easy in Normandy because of the frequent ferries that ply back and forth between the English and French coasts. Cheeses are an obvious choice, with Camembert, Pontilnec, and a range of their cousins like Reblochon, available anywhere from specialist cheese shops to the backs of vans pulled up in lay-bys. Apple products, both liquid and solid, are a great idea, and so too is the honey produced from the flowers of the orchards. It is also worth looking for some of the marvellous unpasteurized cream that is sometimes on sale at farm shops – dark golden with the sort of flavour that you had forgotten could exist if you are used to our anaemic and pasteurized creams.

Crevettes à l'Honfleur
PRAWNS HONFLEUR

Serves 4

100g/4oz button mushrooms

225g/8oz cooked, shelled prawns, defrosted if frozen

300ml/10fl oz Hollandaise sauce

50g/2oz grated cheese – Gruyère is what the natives use, even though it is not a Normandy cheese, or a good rich ripe Cheddar

Honfleur is the great fishing port at the mouth of the Seine, where the Impressionist painters used to come to paint because of the incredible quality of the light. It's also famous for the quality of its fish restaurants on the quay, which is where I first came across this recipe. It uses a generous quantity of Hollandaise Sauce (see p. 118), which you can buy ready-made if you don't feel like making it yourself!

Wash and slice the button mushrooms finely, and place them at the bottom of 4 ramekin dishes. Drain the prawns and mix them with the Hollandaise sauce. Spoon them into the ramekin dishes over the mushrooms. Sprinkle the cheese over the top of the prawns. Put the ramekins under a preheated medium grill, at a distance of about 5–7cm/2–3 inches until the cheese melts and bubbles and the sauce is heated through, about 3–5 minutes. Don't put the ramekins too close to the heat or the cheese will have burned before the sauce is hot. The mushrooms will also be hot, but they will still be crisp. Serve with plenty of crusty French bread to scoop up the wonderful creamy, cheesy, lemony prawny sauce!

Potage Bonne Femme

Serves 4

225g/8oz each of leeks, potatoes, carrots and onions

25g/1oz butter

1 tablespoon chopped parsley

1.2l/2 pints chicken stock (home-made or stock cube), or water

Salt and pepper

This is a classic French soup – the Good Woman's Soup. It is easy to cook – just be careful not to make it too smooth. There should be a little texture left in the vegetables.

Trim the leeks and wash thoroughly. Clean and peel the rest of the vegetables and cut them all into 2.5cm/1 inch chunks. Melt the butter in a nice big saucepan until it is hot but not brown. Add the vegetables and fry in the butter over a fairly high heat until sizzling and golden. Add the salt and pepper – this gives a much more intense flavour than adding seasonings after the liquid – then put in the stock or water. Simmer gently for 15–20 minutes. Older recipes tell you to simmer for an hour and a half. Do not do it – it destroys all the vitamins and a lot of the flavour!

When the vegetables are soft, either mash gently with a fork or process quickly in a food processor or liquidizer until all lumps have gone but the vegetables still have a little texture. If you need to, reheat gently, and serve this lovely creamy soup in bowls with fresh, green parsley sprinkled on top. Lots of hot French bread or toasted granary bread is perfect with this.

Entrecôte Gaillard
STEAK GAILLARD

In Normandy, high over the Seine, there's a great ruin which is called Château Gaillard, or the 'saucy castle'. It was built by Richard I – Richard the Lionheart – to hold back the French who were trying to reclaim Normandy from the English. It didn't work! But today, at the bottom of the hill, there's a little inn where I first had steak cooked like this. Gaillard is a wonderful word – it means merry, hearty, jovial, as well as saucy – I think entirely a suitable name for this dish.

Trim the fat and any gristle off the steaks, or alternatively you can slash them to stop them curling. In a large frying pan into which all the steaks will fit, heat the butter until it foams and fry the steaks briefly on each side. They'll take about 1½ minutes on the first side, and 2 minutes on the second side for rare, an additional 1 minute for medium – and another ½ minute for ruined. Mix the cornichons and onion or shallots with the capers. Add them to the pan when you turn the steaks over. They will be hot through when the steaks are ready.

Remove the steaks and put them on to hot plates and pile the bits from the pan on top. Deglaze the pan by pouring in the vinegar and letting it bubble to get rid of the sharp vinegariness, then add the water and stir all the crusty bits into the liquid. Bring to the boil and let it bubble for about 30 seconds until it becomes a bit syrupy. Pour it over the steaks and serve immediately with plain boiled potatoes sprinkled with fresh parsley with a knob of butter on top. This is a brilliant combination of the richness of the steak, the robust, almost mustard-like sharpness of the sauce and the smoothness of the boiled potatoes.

Serves 4

4 entrecôte steaks, about 175–225g/6–8oz each

50g/2oz butter

50g/2oz cornichons – the little French pickled gherkins, finely chopped

1 small onion or 2 shallots, peeled and finely chopped

25g/1oz capers

4 tablespoons each cider vinegar and water

Faisan à la Vallée d'Auge
PHEASANT VALLÉE D'AUGE

Serves 4

2½ tablespoons butter

1 cock pheasant, jointed

300ml/10fl oz apple juice

Salt and freshly ground black pepper

Bouquet garni of 1 stick celery, 1 bay leaf, a sprig of thyme and 4 sprigs parsley, or use a shop-bought sachet

1 tablespoon cornflour

150ml/5fl oz double cream

2 eating apples

Chopped fresh parsley

The combination of flavours in this dish is marvellous. The Vallée d'Auge lies in the heart of the cider-producing district of northern Normandy and is famous for producing some of the best Calvados – the cider brandy. It is also famous for its pheasants, apples and cream – and this wonderful dish which combines all 3.

In a large deep-sided frying pan or large saucepan, melt 2 tablespoons of the butter and fry the pheasant pieces until golden brown. Pour in the apple juice, season generously and add the bouquet garni. Simmer on top of the stove for 25 minutes. Stir the cornflour into the cream, then pour the mixture into the pan. Blend the sauce thoroughly and heat gently until it thickens.

Core the apples, but don't peel them, and cut each into 12 slices. Melt the remaining butter in a separate pan and turn the apples for a minute or 2 until they turn a very pale gold. Arrange them in a fan shape on serving plates, add the pheasant, and spoon the wonderful creamy, appley sauce around it. Don't forget to remove the bouquet garni. Sprinkle the chopped fresh parsley over the top.

Canard aux Pommes et Beurre
DUCK WITH BUTTERED APPLE RINGS

Serves 4

2 large or 4 smallish duck breasts

50g/2oz butter

Salt and freshly ground black pepper

2 eating apples – Cox's, Spartans or any good, crisp eating apple

2 tablespoons redcurrant jelly

120ml/4fl oz double cream

Ducks, apples, butter and cream are some of the gastronomic stars of Normandy. You must use good, crisp eating apples for this – cooking apples, which in any event the French do not have, have much too soft a texture.

Put the duck breasts on a flat surface and cover them with a piece of greaseproof paper. Beat them gently with the back of a heavy frying pan just to flatten them slightly, as if you were flattening a steak. Remove the paper, then, in the same frying pan (reversed!), heat half the butter, put the duck breasts in, skin side down, and fry them gently for about 5 minutes until the skin is quite crisp. Turn them over, season generously and let them cook gently for about 10–15 minutes. Some people like their duck almost raw or rare. I am not a great fan of that; I don't like them rock hard, but I prefer them brown rather than red.

Take the duck breasts out of the pan and keep them warm. Core the apples and cut them into rings. Heat the rest of the butter in the pan and put in the apple rings. Fry in the foaming butter for 2–3 minutes until they are hot but have not started to disintegrate. Take the rings out and keep warm. Add to the pan the redcurrant jelly and the cream and let them melt together over a moderate heat to make the sauce. Meanwhile, cut each duck breast across the grain into slices and arrange in a fan shape on each plate. Put the apple rings around them in a nice pattern and pour the sauce over the top. The buttered apple rings have the most amazingly intense flavour and the duck breasts are rich and sumptuous, as is the sauce.

Eglefin Dieppoise
HADDOCK DIEPPOISE

Haddock Dieppoise is a marvellous composition of white fish and shellfish. In Dieppe they often use mussels as well as prawns. You can also use plaice or even sole fillets instead of haddock. There are 2 main tricks to this dish – don't cook the fish for too long, and do make sure the sauce is nice and thick, otherwise the juices from the fish thin it down and turn the sauce into a runny gravy.

Make the Béchamel sauce first. Put the milk into a non-stick saucepan and whisk in the flour or cornflour until it is thoroughly blended with the milk. Add the butter and bring gently to the boil, whisking every minute or so. It doesn't need constant whisking, but you must pay attention as soon as the sauce starts to thicken. When it has fully thickened and is just bubbling, turn the heat right down and whisk thoroughly for a smooth, silky texture. Add the nutmeg and season to taste with salt.

Pour one-third of the sauce into a gratin or baking dish. Lay the haddock fillets in a single layer on the sauce and sprinkle with the prawns and button mushrooms. Mix the cream and lemon juice into the remaining sauce and pour on top of the fish and mushrooms. Tuck in the bay leaf and bake in a medium oven at 180°C/160°C fan/350°F/ Gas Mark 4, or the bottom of an Aga roasting oven, for 25–30 minutes until the top is just golden and bubbling. Serve with lots of mashed potatoes to mop up the wonderful sauce.

Serves 4

4 haddock fillets, about 175g/6oz each

100g/4oz peeled prawns

100g/4oz button mushrooms, halved

2 tablespoons double cream

Juice of ½ lemon

1 bay leaf

For the Béchamel sauce:

225ml/8fl oz milk

1 tablespoon plain flour or cornflour, sieved

25g/1oz butter

Pinch of freshly grated nutmeg

Salt

Normandy
cheeseboard
(page 72)

Navets et Carottes Glacés
GLAZED TURNIPS AND CARROTS

Serves 4

225g/8oz carrots, preferably organic

225g/8oz turnips, no larger than 5–8cm/ 2–3 inches across (2 medium turnips)

½ teaspoon salt

1 teaspoon caster sugar

1 tablespoon butter

A little chopped fresh parsley

1 teaspoon white wine or cider vinegar

The French eat vegetables differently from us. Rather than having meat and 3 veg, they cook 1 vegetable or vegetable dish very specifically for the meat or fish they've prepared. The turnips and carrots in this marvellously coloured glossy dish should be small, young and tender.

The carrots and turnips are cooked separately, to start with. Peel the carrots and cut them into chunks about 4cm/1½ inches long and 1cm/½ inch across. Peel the turnips and cut them into quarters. Put the carrots and turnips into separate medium-sized saucepans and just cover them with water. On to the carrots put half the salt and all the sugar. On to the turnips put the butter and the rest of the salt. Bring them both to the boil, turn down and simmer. Do not cover. After about 8–10 minutes, the water will have almost evaporated and the vegetables will be just cooked, but still with a bit of bite in them.

Add the turnips and any remaining water to the saucepan with the carrots (or the other way round!), mix them together and bring to the boil. The butter and the sugar combine to make a kind of caramelized glaze which holds together the marvellous combination of flavours. Put the vegetables into a serving dish and sprinkle a little fresh chopped parsley over the top. For the proper Normandy version of this, pour the vinegar into the pan, swill it round and, as you bring it to the boil, stir in all the bits left in the pan, then pour it over the vegetables. If

---

NORMANDY CHEESEBOARD

Some of the best cheeses in the world come from Normandy, and happily quite a number have found their way over here: Pont l'Evêque and Camembert and Brillat-Savarin and Neufchâtel and Livarot – all are well known outside France. Many are made with at least double cream, so they have a high fat content and are not really to be recommended for anyone on a diet. But they're OK for the rest of us and their rich, creamy

smoothness is a marvellous treat. Together they make a good, balanced cheese-board.

For a firm cheese, Pont l'Evêque is ideal. It isn't hard, like Cheddar, but it is much more solid than Brie. It has a golden rind and it is of medium texture, flavour and intensity.

Livarot is one of the oldest of Normandy cheeses. It is a soft, smooth cows' milk cheese with a lovely full flavour and distinctive smell. The

washed rind is brownish-red. Like many other fine cheeses, it is seasonal, at its best from November to June.

Camembert is one of the most robust of cheeses. It suffers, as Cheddar does, from rather poor copies, but the real Normandy Camembert, strong and ripe, is for the true cheese lover.

For pure indulgence, it is hard to beat the soft, white Brillat-Savarin, full of rich creaminess.

you are serving this with Steak Gaillard (see p. 67), you may prefer not to use the vinegar as you already have some in the steak sauce.

Crêpes Pommes Jacques
APPLE JACQUES PANCAKES

Crêpes Pommes Jacques are cooked with the grated apple filling already mixed into the batter. It gives a lovely, unexpected texture to these pancakes. Topped with cream or crème fraîche they are just marvellous.

In a large bowl mix the flour, sugar, beaten egg, oil and salt together. Beat in the orange juice to make a thick cream, then add the grated apple. Heat the oil in a heavy-based frying pan and drop tablespoons of the mixture into it when it is really hot. You can get 2 or 3 spoonfuls in at a time. Cook for 2–3 minutes, then turn them over and brown the other side. Serve them hot, either singly or sandwiched together with butter, apricot jam or honey. You could also spoon a little cream or crème fraîche over the top.

Serves 6

100g/4oz plain flour, sifted

50g/2oz caster sugar

1 egg, beaten

1 tablespoon vegetable oil

Pinch of salt

200ml/7fl oz orange juice

1 large cooking apple, cored and grated

Oil for frying

Tartes aux Pommes et Mûres
APPLE AND BLACKBERRY TARTS

Normandy is famed for its apples and the various products which it makes from them, while blackberries (or *mûres* – literally, things that grow against the wall) are as common in season in Normandy as they are here. You can buy, in supermarkets, little 7.5cm/3 inch tart cases made of butter shortbread which are seriously wonderful! You can bake your own tart cases, if you prefer, using the recipe for Pâte Sablée (see p. 49). You can also make this as one big tart, but I like the private delight of an individual pudding. The apples should be English eating apples, which have such a marvellous flavour and crispness.

Core and halve the apples, but don't peel them. Grate them finely. In a large, non-stick pan heat the butter and cook the grated apples, turning them over a high heat until they are golden and fragrant. That will only take about 1½ minutes. Add the sugar, the blackberries and the spices and stir them together for about 1 minute, until the sugar melts and the blackberries are hot through. Pile it all into the pastry cases, with some of the blackberries on top, and eat either hot with cream, or even custard (though the French would never serve them with that), or allow them to cool and serve as a marvellous tea-time treat.

Serves 4

4 English eating apples, Cox's or Spartans or something similar

50g/2oz butter

50g/2oz caster sugar

225g/8oz blackberries, fresh or frozen, but not tinned

Pinch each ground cloves and cinnamon

1 × 20cm/8 inch or 4 individual 7.5cm/3 inch pastry flan shells, either bought ready-made or baked blind

BORDEAUX AND THE BEARN

The south-west coast of France has a unique geography and reputation. It is best known for the hundreds of miles of white sandy beaches pounded by Atlantic rollers, stretching from the pine-fringed Landes in the north through the great wine city of Bordeaux to the elegant splendours of Biarritz and Hendaye on the Spanish border. It is the part of France that looks least towards Paris, straining rather across the ocean towards the west and south to the Basque country. In fact, there are as many French Basques as there are Spanish, but the passion for independence doesn't seem to have taken root north of the border as it has in the south. For the rest, this is an area that still thinks of itself as under the old ducal title of Aquitaine. The people of Gascony, in particular, are known to be independent of mind and of politics. And the reputation of the food is second to none. Indeed, many of the standard names for classic French dishes come from this region, *sauce béarnaise* and *entrecôte bordelaise* to name but two.

The raw ingredients of the region are equally famous: tomatoes from Marmande; ham from Bayonne; *foie gras* from the whole area; and truffles from Périgueux are all benchmarks of quality. It is often said that France is divided into three regions by the fat used in cooking: butter in the North, olive oil in the South, and goose fat in the South-West. Although geese are used less now than they used to be, they are still one of the dominant flavours in the fat of the region, and also preserved as a *confit*. This is salted then baked in earthenware jars and added to bean dishes or simply heated through and eaten without the fat that has preserved it. The fat itself is so tasty that it is used to make pastry, even for sweet dishes, and makes a wonderful base for sautéed potatoes.

With such a long coastline, there is inevitably a wide range of fish dishes, particularly in the Arcachon region. Oysters, usually eaten ice cold and raw, are accompanied by sizzling hot sausages which are spicy, as is much of the food from Arcachon south to the Spanish border. Red peppers abound, in varying degrees of pungency. Some are mild like our sweet peppers, but by the time you near the border you encounter peppers of such pungency that they would be called

Opposite: Geese are a familiar sight in Bordeaux and the Béarn, where they are raised to produce foie gras and confits.

chillies anywhere else. Mushrooms, particularly ceps, play a large part in the cuisine, and there are various recipes for cooking them with oil, garlic and herbs, especially for grand feasts.

Except for garlic, some asparagus and the pumpkin family, vegetables are not highly regarded or much grown in the area, and it is possible to go through an entire meal of five or six courses without seeing anything very green. The fruit, on the other hand, is excellent, with white-fleshed nectarines, fine melons and a variety of black grapes flavoured with muscatel being local specialities.

In the great city of Bordeaux there are many restaurants and charming cafés, particularly in the old quarter near the ancient belfry, the *befroi*, and the beautiful theatre designed in the eighteenth century. The steaks in these establishments are excellent, particularly *entrecôte bordelaise*, a steak grilled with beef marrow and flavoured with shallots as a topping. Further south, private homes are places where the traditions of the region are best maintained – some of them quite modern traditions. I can remember a wonderful summer barbecue of duck breast steaks, *magrets de canard*, with the steak cooked almost black on the outside but pink and succulent on the inside. It was eaten with delicious Marmande tomatoes split and cooked extremely slowly with a stuffing of cheese and fresh basil. It is in this region, too, that toast has caught on more than in the rest of France: at breakfast-time in the area around the great inland bay at Arcachon the previous night's bread is cut lengthways and lightly toasted in a form called *tartines*. These are meant to be dipped in a big bowl of *café au lait* before being consumed, although this does take some courage in a smart restaurant.

If you are travelling in the region, be sure to visit the coast with its extraordinary sand dunes and miles of empty beaches. These are very different from the normal image of the French seaside, and you have to be prepared to hike a long way through soft sand to get the benefit of the view or to swim. In the fishing villages dotted along the coast there are welcoming *auberges* which are particularly good at selling the local seafood. For shopping there is a strong taste for the alcoholic products of the area, which include not only the wines of Bordeaux and the Gironde but also Armagnac and the liqueur Marie Brizzard. It is also worth buying a tin, or better still a glass jar, of pure *confit d'oie*, made of goose fat or the lightly cheaper canard. Make sure these *confits* are in their pure form, not simply pork fat flavoured with a little duck or goose. If you can find them, buy fresh truffles when you are in the Périgueux region. They cost a fortune but will keep until you get home. In the season there are also chestnuts, both in their fresh form and in one of their many preserved forms, which include *marrons glacés* or candied chestnuts.

Pâté de Canard
DUCK PÂTÉ

The southern part of western France – the Béarn, and Bordeaux, its northern marcher town – is famous for its ducks and geese. This is a lovely pâté with a rich country flavour. It is easy to make, but you do need a processor, or else a butcher who is willing to do all the mincing for you. It is delectable and sumptuous and very much for a special occasion.

Mince together the duck breast, veal and livers until you have a reasonably smooth purée. Add the garlic, together with the herbs and season generously. Pour in the orange juice and add the rind. Mix in the butter and spoon the whole lot into a 25cm/10 inch loaf tin, about 5cm/2 inches deep. Bake the whole thing in a bain marie – that's a baking tin with 2.5cm/1 inch water in it – for 1 hour at 180°C/160° fan/350°F/Gas Mark 4, or the bottom of an Aga roasting oven. When it's cooked it will shrink away from the sides. Allow it to cool with a light weight on it, like a tin or 2 of tomatoes. When it's cool, take it out and slice like a loaf to serve.

Serves 12

225g/8oz duck breast

225g/8oz pie veal

225g/8oz calf's liver or duck and chicken livers

1 clove garlic, peeled and finely chopped

1 teaspoon each freeze-dried thyme and sage

Salt and pepper

Juice and grated rind of 1 orange

50g/2oz butter

Poivrons Sautés en Salade
COOKED PEPPER SALAD

Peppers are a great feature of cooking in this region, particularly red ones. Peppers are very versatile. They become softer and sweeter when cooked. This recipe makes either a main course salad, a starter, or a great accompaniment to whatever else you are eating – grilled meat, fish or a cold buffet.

Wash the peppers, halve them lengthwise, scrape out all the seeds and white bits, and cut them into 5mm/¼ inch strips. Heat the olive oil in a frying pan with the garlic. Add the peppers and fry gently for 15 minutes, turning regularly. Allow to cool, then transfer the peppers to a serving bowl. Squeeze the lemon over the top, season and add the parsley. Mix gently, then chill for 2 hours before serving.

Serves 4

2 red peppers

2 yellow peppers

2 green peppers

4 tablespoons olive oil

1 clove garlic, peeled and chopped

1 lemon

Salt and pepper

1 tablespoon chopped fresh parsley

Cooked
Pepper Salad
(page 77)
Grilled Sardines
(page 82)

Boeuf en Daube
CASSEROLE OF BEEF

Serves 4

900g/2lb chuck steak

2 tablespoons oil or beef dripping

2 cloves garlic, peeled and chopped

1 onion, peeled and chopped

3 tablespoons red wine vinegar

250ml/8fl oz water

Bouquet garni of 1 stalk celery, 2 stalks parsley, 1 bay leaf and a sprig of thyme, or a shop-bought sachet

1 tablespoon plain flour

1 tablespoon butter

A daube traditionally is meat braised very slowly for several hours, until it is unbelievably tender and delicious. The meat could either be a whole joint, or cut into pieces. It is common to the southern regions of France, where each province adds its own special touch. In this wonderful wine-growing region, the original recipes would have used a glass or two of good wine. I prefer to use a very good red wine vinegar, which is a local alternative.

Cut the meat into 4cm/1½ inch cubes. In a large casserole, heat the oil or beef dripping and quickly brown the meat. Add the garlic and onion, and fry until they just start to brown. Pour in the wine vinegar and deglaze. You do this by turning up the heat and using the vinegar to scrape up the brown bits on the bottom of the casserole. When the liquid has almost evaporated, add the water and the bouquet garni. The liquid should come about halfway up the meat. Cover and cook in a low oven at 150°C/140°C fan/ 300°F/Gas Mark 2 for 1½–2 hours. You can stir this casserole once during cooking to make sure all the meat remains moist.

When the meat is cooked, take the casserole out of the oven. Mash the flour and butter together until they make a smooth paste and add this, teaspoon by teaspoon, to the casserole, preferably over a gentle heat, allowing each teaspoon to dissolve and mix in before adding the next. The sauce will turn glossy and thick and will just coat the meat. Remove the bouquet garni and serve.

Confit d'Oie
CONFIT OF GOOSE

Confit of goose is just bits of goose preserved in goose fat. It will keep in a cool place for up to 6 months. The French use it to enrich slow-cooked country dishes, like cassoulet. Goose is expensive, so unless you have a lot of goose left over from a roast bird, this can be a bit of an indulgence, but it is a good way of using up the leftovers.

Cut the goose into moderate-sized pieces and place in preserving jars. Cover with goose fat and a teaspoon of coarse salt per jar. Bake in a medium oven at 180°C/160°C fan/350°F/Gas Mark 4, or the bottom of an Aga roasting oven, for 30 minutes. Make sure all the meat is under fat before the jars cool and you seal them. To use the confit, stand the jar in a pan of boiling water until the fat melts. Fish out the pieces of goose and add to soups, stews or cassoulets. You can even grill them and eat them on their own. Store the rest by allowing the fat to harden again and resealing the jar.

Serves 4

Left-over goose meat

Goose fat

1 teaspoon coarse salt
per jar

HOW TO MAKE BÉARNAISE SAUCE

Béarnaise sauce was created in the 1830s in a restaurant in St Germain-en-Laye by a chef from the South-West. It is traditionally served with grilled meat or fish. Sauces that are emulsions of eggs and butter are notoriously difficult to make successfully – or at least they were before the advent of the food processor. This basic recipe is slightly different and the result slightly lighter than the traditional hand-beaten recipes, but it tastes delicious and it's foolproof!

Method:
In a small saucepan, bring the wine vinegar to the boil with the finely chopped shallot and tarragon, then strain and discard the herb and shallot. Put the eggs and egg yolk, a pinch of salt, and the tarragon and shallot flavoured vinegar into the bowl of a liquidizer or food processor. Cut the butter into chunks, put it into a saucepan and heat gently until the butter has completely melted and foams. As soon as it hisses and gives off steam, switch on the machine and beat the eggs thoroughly. With the motor running, pour the butter in a steady stream on to the egg mixture. Don't pour in the white residue at the bottom of the saucepan – tip this away but don't rinse the pan. Switch off the motor and pour the sauce back into the saucepan, stirring gently but continuously off the heat. Within 30 seconds, the sauce will have thickened even more and it is ready to serve. It can be kept warm in a bowl over a pan of hot water for up to 10 minutes, but no more.

For 300ml/10fl oz:

1 tablespoon wine vinegar

1 teaspoon each chopped
shallot and fresh tarragon

2 eggs and 1 egg yolk

Salt

225g/8oz lightly salted
butter

Foies de Volaille Sautés aux Raisins
CHICKEN LIVERS SAUTÉED WITH GRAPES

Serves 4 as a main course or 8 as a starter

450g/1lb chicken livers, fresh or frozen

1 tablespoon each butter and olive oil

180ml/6fl oz chicken stock, home-made or stock cube

1 teaspoon arrowroot

Salt and freshly ground black pepper

100g/4oz seedless grapes

In the South-West of France, this recipe is usually made with the wonderful duck livers which are readily available there. Here it is very difficult to buy them at all, and if you do find any, they tend to be very expensive. The combination of chicken livers and grapes is very delicious and makes a marvellous starter or main course.

Thaw the chicken livers if necessary and trim them. In a medium-sized frying pan, melt the butter in the oil. Sauté the chicken livers over a medium heat briefly. Mix together the chicken stock and arrowroot and pour into the frying pan. Turn up the heat to bring the liquid to the boil, then turn the heat down so it just simmers for 3–4 minutes. Check for seasoning, add the grapes to the pan, stir briefly, then serve immediately. Fluffy rice goes well with this for a main course, or crusty French bread if you are serving it as a starter.

Sardines Grillées
GRILLED SARDINES

Serves 4

8 medium-sized sardines, trimmed and gutted

25g/1oz sea salt

2 tablespoons olive oil

1 large lemon

The sardines from the French Atlantic coast are quite wonderful – silvery skinned, plump fleshed and with a very fine flavour. Locally they are either fried or grilled. I prefer sardines grilled until their skins are light and crisp – surely one of life's great delights! Like many simple dishes, it is the flavour and freshness of the raw ingredients that makes all the difference. Most fishmongers and supermarket fish counters now sell sardines. They are about the size of small herrings, but the taste is very different: the darker the flesh, the more intense the flavour. Line the grill pan with silver foil before you cook. It makes the cleaning a lot easier, but it also reflects the heat up on to the fish so they cook more quickly.

Rub the sardines with the salt and leave for 10 minutes. Wash the salt off thoroughly, allow the sardines to dry on kitchen paper, and then wipe them all over with the olive oil. Heat the grill to maximum for at least 10 minutes before you want to cook the sardines. Lightly oil the rack so that the fish doesn't stick, and place the sardines on it. The fish should be about 4–5cm/1½–2 inches away from the grill. Cook them for 2–3 minutes on 1 side, then turn them and cook for another 2 minutes on the other side. The skin may char slightly, but the flesh should be firm and not burnt. Remove from the grill and squeeze the lemon over them immediately. Serve while they are hot.

Haricots Verts Amandine
FRENCH BEANS WITH ALMONDS

Serves 4

350g/12oz little string beans, topped and tailed (see method)

25g/1oz butter

50g/2oz slivered almonds

Salt and freshly ground black pepper

Almonds in southern France ripen in May and to eat them sweet and fresh off the tree is a great delight. They go wonderfully well with vegetables, and the pale gold of the almonds and bright green of the beans looks very pretty too.

This is quite a heap of beans to top and tail, so here is the Crafty way of doing it: Wash the beans, take a handful of them and hold them vertically over a chopping board. Shake them gently in your hand until they slip down so the tip of each bean just touches the surface of the board. When they're all level, lay them flat and cut off the ends. Now turn them round and repeat the process for the other ends.

When you've trimmed them all, put the beans into a saucepan of boiling water and cook for 6–8 minutes, depending on thickness, until they are still bright green but cooked through. Drain well and set aside. Put the butter into a hot pan and, when it has melted, add the almonds and fry until they are light golden. Add the beans, turn them briskly for 1 minute, season, then serve.

Casserole of Beef
(page 80)
French Beans with
Almonds (page 83)

Clafoutis

Serves 4

5 eggs

150g/5oz each of icing sugar and plain flour

1 tablespoon oil

450g/1lb fresh black cherries or cooking apples

50g/2oz caster sugar

1 teaspoon cinnamon, if using apples

There is no direct translation of clafoutis, just exclamations of delight as it is eaten! Traditionally, it is a big pancake, filled with the huge, wonderful fresh black cherries of the region. Whether you stone the cherries or not is up to you. If you don't, just remember to warn your guests first! When black cherries aren't available, it is often made with other fruit, apples being a particularly delicious alternative.

You can either do this by hand or use a food processor. If you are making it by hand, you need a nice big bowl. Break the eggs into it and whisk them. Add a tablespoon of flour and a tablespoon of icing sugar, and whisk in and keep doing that until all the flour and sugar is used up. You should now have a nice thick creamy batter. Add the oil.

If you are using a food processor put in the eggs, icing sugar and flour and whizz until the thick batter has formed. Add the oil. If you are using cherries, remove the stalks, wash them and sprinkle them with the caster sugar. If you're using apples, peel, core and cut them into walnut-sized pieces and mix with the cinnamon and sugar.

Pour the batter into a long, greased gratin or baking dish, about 4cm/1½ inches deep and about 30cm/12 inches long, then put the cherries or apples on top. Put the dish into a medium oven for about 1 hour at 180°C/160°C fan/350°F/Gas Mark 4, or the bottom of an Aga roasting oven. The pancake rises golden around the fruit. Serve with cream or fromage frais.

BORDEAUX AND BEARN CHEESEBOARD

This western part of France is dominated by the sea, mountains and rivers. From the green, vine-covered hills and valleys of Bordeaux, to the looming Pyrenees, the produce of this region is marvellous. Not all of the cheeses produced here travel well, so your choice is limited and you will need to augment your cheeseboard with a good, crumbly goats' cheese.

In the northern part, round the Dordogne, Chaumes is made. It is a lovely, smooth, creamy cheese with quite a marked flavour and an orange-coloured rind. It is a familiar sight in our supermarkets.

Fromage des Pyrénées can also be found in this country. It has either a black or brown wax rind, covering a semi-hard cows' milk cheese, pale yellow in colour, with little

holes. The flavour is quite pronounced.

If you are planning a summer holiday in the region, you must try the traditional ewes' milk cheeses, with a delicate, nutty flavour and a yellow rind. These are farmhouse cheeses, made for local consumption, and for the tourist lucky enough to come across them. They don't travel well, so make the most of them while you can!

Pain aux Noix
WALNUT BREAD

The French bake wonderful bread, with a huge variety of textures and tastes. One of my favourites is this walnut bread from the South-West. It is a small, chewy loaf, often with a dark brown crust and richly studded with walnuts. The slightly sweet and chewy texture goes marvellously with cheese, and it is also a delight eaten on its own, with just a little good butter. This recipe makes 2 medium-sized loaves which will keep for 4 or 5 days. Once they have completely cooled, keep them loosely wrapped in a plastic bag.

Serves 4

25g/1oz fresh yeast

1 tablespoon soft dark brown sugar

450ml/15fl oz warm water

350g/12oz unbleached strong white bread flour

350g/12oz wholemeal bread flour

½ teaspoon salt

3 tablespoons walnut oil

100g/4oz shelled walnuts

Put the yeast in a bowl and add just a pinch of the sugar and 120ml/4fl oz of the warm water. Stir until thoroughly blended, then leave for 10 minutes until frothy. Mix the white and wholemeal flours together and add the salt and walnut oil. When the yeast has frothed, add it to the flour with most of the remaining warm water and knead together until you have a resilient, elastic dough. Don't add all the water, keep a little back and see how much water the flour will absorb. Put the dough aside to rise in a warm place under a cloth for 45–50 minutes. It should comfortably double in size.

Knock it down with the back of your hand and knead again briefly, adding the rest of the sugar and three-quarters of the walnuts, which you can crush lightly in your hand as you knead. Divide the dough in 2 and shape into 2 large rolls or cushion shapes, or you can put them into 2 greased 450g/1lb loaf tins. Stud the loaves with the remaining walnuts and put them to rise on a baking tray in a warm place covered with a cloth for 30–40 minutes until fully risen.

Bake the loaves in a hot oven at 210°C/190°C fan/425°F/Gas Mark 7, or the top of an Aga roasting oven, for 25 minutes. Reduce the temperature to 180°C/160°C fan/350°F/Gas Mark 4, or the bottom of an Aga roasting oven, and bake for another 20–25 minutes until the bottom sounds hollow when you tap it. Remove to a wire rack and allow to cool completely before slicing and eating.

ALSACE-LORRAINE

lthough they are almost always mentioned in the same breath, Alsace and Lorraine are really two very different regions; indeed Lorraine has only recently become a part of France. The birthplace of France's greatest hero, Joan of Arc, Lorraine was until nearly the end of the eighteenth century an independent duchy – but one always closely allied to her great neighbour to the west. Alsace, on the other hand, was for many years a part of France until 1871 when, on Bismarck's consolidating of the German Empire, it was annexed; Alsace remained a part of Germany until after World War I. Both regions are situated at the north-eastern corner of France and are thus very much a part of central Europe in their climate and geography – strongly agricultural and with little contact with the products of the sea. In recent times they have both assumed new importance with the growth of the European Union: Strasbourg, the capital of Alsace, has become one of the three great European centres of the Union, while Nancy, the capital of Lorraine, is an ever-growing industrial centre situated close to the great markets of Germany and northern Europe.

In culinary terms, too, the provinces differ greatly from each other despite their proximity. Each provides French cuisine with one of the great dishes of the world: *quiche lorraine*, and *foie gras* from Alsace. Pastry and baking is one of the few common themes in the cooking of both, and in addition to the eponymous pastry tart filled with a bacon-flavoured savoury egg custard there are quiches in Lorraine made of many ingredients – the most famous of which is probably the one filled with onions and cream, which I must admit is my personal favourite. Not all the baking is savoury. With an amazing range of cakes and specialities, it is Lorraine where *madeleines* were first invented. These are the classic little French cakes, shaped like plump biscuits, that evoked a literary passion in Proust, who used them to trigger his memories of things past. Rum babas also come from this area and were the favourite of the last Duke of Lorraine. This duke also happened to be King of Poland and built the exquisite eighteenth-century Place Stanislaus in the centre of Nancy which still stands untampered with to this day.

The highly controversial *foie gras* is firmly positioned at the heart of Alsace. Made from the livers of force-fed geese, and now very often ducks, there is no question that *foie gras* is in itself delectable, albeit

Opposite: The beautiful village church at Hunawihr, Alsace.

extremely rich. However, the discomfort suffered by the geese for this benefit now makes it off limits to all of us for whom animal welfare is an issue. There are, however, many other pâtés to be enjoyed in this region – one of the great pâté-making areas of France. They can be made not only from geese but also from duck and game. There's a lot of game cooked in Alsace, often in the German style with cream sauces and served with big flat noodles known as spaetsle. Poultry dishes are also popular, and many recipes are built around the region's succulent chicken. This includes an increasingly rare but delicious chicken dish cooked with river crayfish in a pale pink creamy sauce.

The countryside of Lorraine is solid, rolling and heavily forested, not orchard country but a place where soft fruits are grown in profusion, particularly around the old capital, Bar-le-Duc; they are then turned into the most famous jams and jellies in France. These are more than just jams, with the red, white and black currants, strawberries and raspberries being made into confitures which are often eaten on their own with a spoonful of cream or one of the pale unsalted cream cheeses known as *coeurs à la crème*. They fetch a formidable price, particularly in some of the fancier Paris shops, but they are certainly worth seeking out when you are in the area. Frequently the soft fruits are made into eau de vie – white fruit-flavoured liqueurs totally dry and heavily scented with raspberries and plums. Lorraine is famous too for its water, Vittel.

Alsace is much more a wine-growing country, and the food reflects its shared German heritage: *choucroute*, or *sauerkraut*, has its French home here, with sausages and a hearty style of eating that goes with it. The dish itself is firmly established on the menus of brasseries all over France, but its home is in the solid centre of Alsace. One small word of warning: beware of what I hope is just a passing trend – that of cooking the region's ubiquitous potato for less long than usual. The ones I tasted were crisp and didn't suit the boiled version at all.

Cheeses match the sense of hearty and rustic eating that covers the whole area of Alsace-Lorraine: Munster, a rich cheese which when fully ripe is as pungent as any in France; and Carré de l'Est, the local equivalent of a Brie or Camembert made in the form of a square six inches across and allowed to ripen and soften just like the cheeses from Normandy. Also to be found locally are a number of cheeses which reflect the local taste for aniseed, known as *anisé*.

Alsace-Lorraine is a part of France mercifully free of the often tourist-led commitment to fast-food eating places. It still abounds with small auberges and hotels where the main meal of the day is served at lunchtime and remains old-fashionedly hearty.

Potage de Carottes
CARROT SOUP

The food in Alsace is hearty, warm and filling, and this is a soup designed to be served in big bowls for hearty appetites! It has something of a surprise ingredient. Turmeric is a bright, golden spice that adds flavour, not heat. You might expect to find it in a curry rather than in a soup from northern France, but in this soup it adds both colour and a warm, subtle flavour. There is one other surprising ingredient, and that is natural yoghurt. I must admit that in Alsace itself, double cream rather than yoghurt would be used, but I have to draw the line somewhere!

Peel the vegetables, cut into chunks and put them all into a large saucepan over a low heat with the oil to stop them sticking. Let them simmer gently for 3–4 minutes, turning them occasionally. Sprinkle in the turmeric and salt and pepper, and turn the vegetables again until thoroughly coated. Add the chicken stock, bring to the boil, then simmer over a medium heat for 20–25 minutes with the lid on the saucepan until all the vegetables are soft.

Remove the vegetables from the saucepan with enough of the stock to make a purée, and either mash with a fork, press through a sieve or (much easier) whizz in a food processor for about 15 seconds until smooth. Pour the purée back into the saucepan and blend in with the remaining stock. Season, heat through and pour into a soup tureen or a large serving bowl. Beat the yoghurt in its pot until it is smooth, then stir it into the golden soup so it swirls into a marbled pattern. The turmeric makes the golden colour even more intense and doesn't actually make it spicy; rather it gives it a more robust, earthy flavour. Serve with lots of brown bread and butter, French bread, or *pain de campagne*, the French equivalent of wholemeal.

Serves 4–6

600g/1¼lb carrots

2 medium-sized potatoes

2 onions

1–2 tablespoons oil

½ teaspoon turmeric

Salt and pepper

900ml/1½ pints chicken stock

1 small carton (5fl oz) natural yoghurt

Choucroute
SAUERKRAUT

Serves 4

700g/1½lb sauerkraut

50ml/2fl oz oil or
50g/2oz butter

350g/12oz onion, peeled
and thinly sliced

1 clove garlic, peeled and
thinly sliced

1 large glass apple juice

8 frankfurters

100g/4oz salami, sliced

Choucroute, or Sauerkraut, makes a very hearty 1-pot meal. It originated in Alsace-Lorraine, though it is now a great classic dish served all over France, from the brasseries of Paris to hostelleries in the Loire. It is a wonderful, rich winter dish and the way the French cook it is quite subtle and sophisticated. Sauerkraut, which is pickled cabbage, is sold in jars in most supermarkets. In France they used to sell it in Alsace from huge barrels, but EC directives have probably stopped that! Traditionally, it is served with boiled potatoes.

Take the sauerkraut out of the jar, put it in a colander and rinse it in cold water for about 30 seconds to get rid of all the salty water around it. Drain it thoroughly. In a large saucepan, heat the oil or butter and fry the onions and garlic together until they turn pale gold. Add the sauerkraut, the apple juice and the frankfurters, which you bury in the sauerkraut, put the lid on and cook over a gentle to medium heat, until the whole thing is just bubbling. Let it simmer gently for about 20 minutes until the frankfurters are cooked and the whole mixture is fragrant.

HOW TO MAKE QUICHE

Serves 4

1 tablespoon butter

225g/8oz onions, peeled and
sliced very thinly

225g/8oz pâte brisée or
shortcrust pastry

150g/5oz finely grated
Gruyère cheese

2 eggs

1 egg yolk

200ml/7fl oz milk

Pinch of freshly grated
nutmeg

Quiche probably originated in Lorraine, where of course the famous one is made from eggs, cream and bacon. But the fillings can be so various that you are really only limited by your own imagination and good taste! The pastry you use is important. You can make quiches from pâte brisée, which is almost the same recipe as pâte sablée (see p. 49). For pâte brisée you omit the sugar and add 25g/1oz more flour. You can also use shortcrust pastry, home-made or bought from your local supermarket. One of my favourite fillings is cheese and onion.

Method:
In a frying pan, melt the butter and fry the onions gently for about 5 minutes until they're soft but not brown. Use the pastry to line a 20cm/8 inch metal flan dish and spread the onion mixture on that. (If you prefer to use a china quiche dish, you need to bake the pastry blind first. Roll out the pastry, line the china dish and prick it all over with a fork. Bake it in a hot oven at 200°C/180°C fan/400°F/Gas Mark 6, or the top of an Aga roasting oven, for about 10 minutes, then lay the onion mixture on it.)

Spoon the cheese over the onions. Beat the eggs, egg yolk and milk together and pour over the top. The mixture should come to about 5mm/¼ inch below the rim. Sprinkle with nutmeg and bake in a pre-heated oven at 220°C/200°C fan/425°F/Gas Mark 7, or the top of an Aga roasting oven, for about 25 minutes. Reduce the temperature to 190°C/170°C fan/375°F/Gas Mark 5, or move the quiche to the middle of an Aga roasting oven, for another 10 minutes until the top is brown and risen and the pastry cooked through. Serve it hot while it still has maximum lift. It is also delicious cold, but it does sink a little.

Cut the slices of salami into very thin matchsticks and, in a small frying pan, quickly fry them in their own fat until crisp. To serve, pile the whole great steaming mass of sauerkraut and frankfurters in a deep dish and sprinkle the salami on top. Surround it with newly boiled potatoes and serve with mustard and gherkins on the side.

Le Civet de Lièvre
JUGGED HARE

Hare is a marvellous, rich meat which deserves a lot more popularity than it has. In France it is eaten much more than here – in fact so much was hunted that the French had to import animals from Hungary to replenish depleted stocks. It makes wonderful pâtés, or you can roast it, or casserole it with chocolate. You should always buy it from a specialist game dealer or butcher – not only will you be sure of the quality, but the meat will be prepared for you in the way you want. One of my favourite recipes is for jugged hare. Although traditionally the blood was saved to thicken the sauce, I really would not do it – it is an unpleasant process and produces a strong, not particularly attractive flavour. Jugged hare goes beautifully with boiled potatoes, Glazed Turnips and Carrots (see p. 72), and Red Cabbage with Apples (see p. 95).

Wash the pieces of hare in cold water and dry on kitchen paper. Put the pieces of hare into a large bowl and season generously with salt, pepper and mace. Then put them into a tall, thin casserole or an ovenproof jug. Add the bouquet garni, beef stock, anchovies and clove-studded onions. Pour in enough water to come almost, but not quite, over the top of the hare, then cover the jug or casserole tightly. Stand it in a baking tray with 5cm/ 2 inches of boiling water and place the whole lot in a lowish oven, 160°C/150°C fan/325°F/Gas Mark 3, or the bottom of the Aga, for 1½–2 hours until the hare is tender.

Remove the pieces of hare and keep warm. Pour the cooking liquid through a sieve into a saucepan, add the cayenne pepper, redcurrant jelly, mustard, and the cornflour mixed to a paste with a little water. Stir together over a gentle heat, bring to the boil and allow to thicken. Place the hare on a serving dish and pour the sauce over it.

Serves 4–6

1 hare, cut into sections

Salt and freshly ground black pepper

1 blade of mace, crushed, or 1 teaspoon ground mace

Bouquet garni of 1 stalk celery, 2 stalks parsley, 1 bay leaf and a sprig of thyme, or a shop-bought sachet

600ml/1 pint beef stock (see p.152) or use a stock cube

2 anchovy fillets

2 onions, peeled and stuck with 4 cloves

Pinch of cayenne pepper

1 tablespoon redcurrant jelly

1 tablespoon made mustard

2 teaspoons cornflour

Cuissot Rôti
MARINATED ROAST HAUNCH OF VENISON

Serves 8

1 haunch of venison,
about 2.25kg/5lb

2 teaspoons cornflour
made into a paste with a
little water

For the marinade:

600ml/1 pint red wine or
acidic juice

225g/8oz carrots, peeled
and sliced

225g/8oz onions, peeled
and sliced

6 juniper berries, crushed

Salt and freshly ground
black pepper

We tend to associate this part of France with hearty eating, but venison makes a very sophisticated dish, as well as a robust one. Haunch of venison is the most expensive cut. It is basically a rear leg and is similar to a leg of lamb. Traditionally it is marinated before cooking for at least 24 hours, and sometimes even 2 or 3 days. In France, red wine is most often used for the marinade, but you can substitute any acidic juice – cranberry or even cloudy apple juice. The aim is to achieve a rich, tender joint of meat.

Mix together the ingredients for the marinade. Put the meat into a deep glass or china bowl – not metal – and pour over the marinade. Leave in a cool place for about 24 hours, turning the meat occasionally. Drain the meat from the marinade, which you can then strain. Keep 150ml/5fl oz for the sauce. Boil and use the rest as the basis for a wonderfully flavoured gravy or sauce.

Put the venison into a baking tray, cover it loosely with buttered foil, and roast in a medium oven, 190°C/170°C fan/375°F/Gas Mark 5, or the bottom of an Aga roasting oven, for 45 minutes per kg/20 minutes per lb plus another 20 minutes. When it is cooked, allow the meat to rest in a warm place for 10–15 minutes.

Make the sauce from the pan drippings and the reserved marinade, thickened with the cornflour paste. Check the sauce for seasoning and balance, then slice the venison as you would a leg of lamb. Serve with a Purée of Celeriac and Potato (see p. 151) and either sprouts or Red Cabbage with Apples (see p. 95).

Oie Rôtie
ROAST GOOSE

Serves 6

1 goose, about
2.75–3kg/6–7lb

1 large Spanish onion,
peeled and chopped

1 tablespoon chopped fresh
sage or ½ tablespoon dried
sage

There is something of a love affair in France with the goose – from the luxury of foie gras, to Confit d'Oie (see p. 81), to cooking with goose fat, which you find quite extensively in this region. The flavour of goose is rich and savoury and is becoming pretty popular here in Britain. Larger supermarkets now stock fresh and frozen geese. Buy a fresh or chilled one, if you can, a frozen one will need 2–3 days to defrost in the fridge. Not more than 12 hours before cooking it, put the fresh or thoroughly defrosted goose into a colander in the sink and pour a kettle of boiling water over it, turning it halfway. This loosens the skin from the flesh and allows the fat to drain away. Let it drain and dry off for 2 hours. This will help crisp the skin and prevent greasiness. If the goose comes with a neat pack of giblets, use them to make the most delicious gravy. In France, very often a roast goose is stuffed and cooked with apples and pears around it. I like it with the apples in the stuffing and also with apple sauce.

Once you have poured the boiling water over the goose, leave it to dry and do not put it back in the fridge. Put the onion, the sage, the breadcrumbs and the black pepper into a bowl. Core but don't peel the Bramleys and rough-chop them. Mix and then bind the whole lot together with the egg. Stuff the cavity of the goose with this – don't cram the stuffing in or it will be pushed out of the end during cooking – so just three-quarters fill it. Don't forget to weigh the goose again after you have stuffed it.

Put the goose on to a rack over a roasting tin. The fat will run out during the cooking and you may need to pour it off as the goose cooks. Roast it at 190°C/170°C fan/375°F/Gas Mark 5, or the middle of an Aga roasting oven, for 45 minutes per kg/20 minutes per lb plus 20 minutes more. Don't overcook it or it will dry out. Serve with Red Cabbage with Apples (see below), roast potatoes, the giblet gravy, apple sauce and, of course, the stuffing.

100g/4oz fresh breadcrumbs

Salt and freshly ground black pepper

225g/8oz Bramley apples

1 egg

Chou Rouge aux Pommes
RED CABBAGE WITH APPLES

Red cabbage with apples is a traditional accompaniment to hare and venison. Its sweet-sour taste beautifully complements the richness of the meat. It is eaten like this in Alsace and Lorraine, and in fact it is popular throughout central Europe.

Remove the stalk from the cabbage, and cut it into 1cm/½ inch slices. Heat the vegetable oil in a flameproof casserole and fry the onion for 5 minutes until soft but not browned. Add the apple slices and cabbage, and toss so everything is coated. Season generously and stir in the cider vinegar, sugar and water. Cover the casserole and bake in a lowish oven at 160°C/150°C fan/325°F/Gas Mark 3, or the bottom of the Aga, for 25 minutes. Take the casserole out of the oven add the cloves and allspice, and mix well. Add a little more water if the cabbage is drying out. Return to the oven for another 25 minutes, then serve at once.

Serves 4

700g/1½lb red cabbage

1 tablespoon vegetable oil

1 onion, peeled and thinly sliced

1 cooking apple, peeled, cored and thinly sliced

Salt and freshly ground black pepper

2 tablespoons cider vinegar

1 tablespoon soft brown sugar

1–2 tablespoons water

Pinch of ground cloves

Pinch of ground allspice

Jugged Hare
(page 93)
Red Cabbage with
Apples (page 95)
Rustic Potatoes
(page 98)

Pommes de Terre Paysanne
RUSTIC POTATOES

Serves 4

700g/1½lb potatoes, preferably Romano or salad potatoes

50g/2oz butter

1 large or 2 medium-sized leeks

120ml/4fl oz double cream

Salt and freshly ground black pepper

40g/1½ oz chopped fresh parsley

The quality of both produce and cooking in Alsace makes even the most simple of dishes superb. It's the part of France where a lot of potato dishes come from and a lot of dishes made with leeks. This recipe is a mixture of the two. I call it Pommes de Terre Paysanne because I first had it in a small hostellerie where the cooking was seriously rustic and they produced this wonderful rich dish. You need yellow potatoes, the ones which don't turn fluffy when cooked and are often sold as salad potatoes. You also need handfuls of fresh parsley, deep green and rich in vitamin C!

Peel the potatoes if you want to, but if the skins are nice and light, keep them on and simply scrub the potatoes. Plunge the potatoes into a big pot of boiling water and blanch them thoroughly for 6–8 minutes. They should only just begin to soften. Drain them and allow them to cool slightly. Slice them thickly into reasonable-sized pieces. Heat the butter in a large pan and fry the potatoes until they start to turn golden. Trim the leeks, slice them down the middle and wash them thoroughly in a big bowl of water to get rid of all the sand and grit. When they're clean, slice them very thinly and add them to the potatoes. Turn it all gently until the potatoes have cooked through and the leeks have softened – they will take about 5 minutes. Pour in the double cream, season generously and swirl it all together. Pile it into a dish and sprinkle with handfuls of chopped parsley before serving. You can serve this with sausages or chops, but I like it just on its own, steaming hot in a big bowl!

ALSACE-LORRAINE CHEESEBOARD

Alsace and Lorraine produce marvellous vegetables, fruit, wines, fish, game and cheese. In fact there is a great tradition of cooking with cheese here, as well as simply eating it! Happily, many of these cheeses travel well and can easily be found in shops here.

The star of Alsatian cheese is Munster, a soft yellow cheese made from cows' milk with a pale orange rind. What is not pale about it is its smell and flavour, both of which are wonderfully pungent. Like Livarot, Pont l'Evêque and Mont d'Or, amongst others, it is washed regularly in warm salty water to develop the rind – which is edible – and the flavour.

One of the most popular exports from here is Carré d'Est, a soft, creamy cheese made in Lorraine and Champagne.

Also widely available in Britain is Morbier, which is made just south of Alsace, in Franche-Comté. It is a pleasant cheese with a modestly pronounced flavour. It has a thin line of ash running horizontally through the middle which separates the curds from the morning milk from those of the evening milk.

Worth trying if you are visiting the region is Géromé which is also made from the milk of cows pastured in the Vosges mountains. It is a soft cheese, pretty pungent when fully ripe. In contrast, Gérardmer, which comes from the same place, is a soft cows' milk cheese with a washed rind and distinctive smell and is always eaten fresh. It is cylinder-shaped and is often called Lorraine or Gros Lorraine.

Jalousie aux Prunes
PLUM JALOUSIE

If this were literally translated, it would be something like 'plum Venetian blind'! A jalousie is a slatted blind which allows just a little sunshine through the windows, but not enough to fade the furnishings inside. The pudding got its name because the pastry on the top is slashed to give it a slatted appearance. Firm, ripe plums make the most marvellous filling. If you can buy those which come from Alsace, then you are in for a great treat.

You need a Swiss roll tin for this, about 30 × 20cm/12 × 8 inches. Roll out two-thirds of the pastry to fit the tin. If you don't have a tin this size, use a larger one and pinch the edges of the pastry – which should still be 30 × 20cm/12 × 8 inches – so they form a small ridge all round to contain the filling. If the plums are canned, drain them, split them and take out the stones and reserve the juice. If the plums are fresh, poach them in a little water with the sugar for 5–10 minutes until they're just cooked. Drain them, reserving the cooking syrup, cut them in half and take out the stones. Arrange the plums (fresh or canned) on the pastry in a pretty pattern.

Add the cinnamon to the reserved syrup and stir in the cornflour. Bring it to the boil until it forms a thick coating syrup. Spoon it carefully over the plums, making sure it doesn't go over the sides of the pastry. To make the window with the jalousie blind, roll out the remaining third of the pastry quite thinly until it is the same width but about half the length of the tart tin (or pastry base). Very carefully slit it across at about ¼ inch intervals, as if you were drawing a Venetian blind on it, making sure you leave a good rim like a picture frame all round it. Pick up the pastry carefully and stretch it gently so that when you lay it over the plums, it just covers them. What happens is that the slits open out into a kind of lattice. There is a special cutter that does this very neatly and simply – try your nearest kitchen shop.

Fasten the edges of the pastry together so they won't separate, and bake the tart in a hot oven at 200°C/180°C fan/400°F/Gas Mark 6, or the top of an Aga roasting oven, for about 35 minutes, until the pastry is golden and puffed and the filling is cooked through. This tart is nicest left to cool, and then served in slices, but you can have it hot, served with cream.

Serves 4

250g/10oz puff pastry, the supermarket kind is fine

350g/12oz plums, fresh are best but you can use good canned plums

50g/2oz sugar (if you are using fresh plums)

1 teaspoon cinnamon

2 teaspoons cornflour

BURGUNDY

Burgundy is a land which demands superlatives. The late Jane Grigson once described it as 'unfairly blessed with the fruits of the earth and of man's skill', and Elizabeth David remarked that the dishes of Burgundy might be said to 'represent the most sumptuous kind of country cooking brought to a point of finesse'. I too have wonderful memories of the food of Burgundy. In a tiny village just south of Dijon there are two separate Michelin-starred restaurants. In one of them, full of locals casually dressed in shorts, their children accompanying them and enjoying the hot summer evening, I was served a meal of casual brilliance: hot chicken liver pâté, local fish, a perfectly cooked piece of beef with a dark rich sauce, and tiny, intensely flavoured forest strawberries served with a purée of raspberries and cream so thick that it was almost like a cheese. It would be a comfort for those of us accustomed to British restaurants to say that the bill matched the standard of the restaurant, but it was almost ridiculously small – only a prepaid villa booking on the coast dragged us away the following day. Burgundy is like that. The people are comfortable and relaxed, and everywhere you turn the countryside and the produce combine to suggest a land of plenty.

The upper reaches of the Loire and the lower reaches of the River Saône, heading for the Atlantic and the Mediterranean respectively, water the land of Burgundy. River fish are a major part of the region's cuisine, cooked and eaten with the dry white wines for which Burgundy is so famous. Over-fishing and pollution have done a great deal of harm to supplies, and a law was passed some years ago preventing the sale of river fish to restaurants; more recently, restocking and the growth in trout-farming has helped increase numbers again and fish has now reappeared on many restaurant menus.

Mustards play a large part in both Burgundian cuisine and commerce, since Dijon is known throughout the world as the mustard capital, with records of mustard-flavoured dishes dating back to Roman times. The mustards come in a variety of forms, from the smooth pale gold of *Dijon* to the strong flavours of the wholegrain *ancienne*.

Beef is a major product of the area, too, with Charolais cattle supposedly producing the best beef in France. The meat is cooked in

Opposite: Beaujolais vineyards near Beaujeu.

the method named after the region itself, *à la bourgignonne*, simmered in the world-famous local red wines and dressed with baby onions and mushrooms. Chickens from Burgundy, *poulets de Bresse*, are also a watchword for quality, as are the great red wines of Mâcon, Beaune and Chambertin. These wines are often drunk with cheeses; indeed, cheeses are an excellent excuse for finishing a bottle of wine. Although many of the local cheeses are not well known outside the immediate area, the Burgundians eat them in quantity, and have even produced one of the great cheese dishes of France, a cheese pastry called *gougère* which is good enough to eat on its own, either as a first or a savoury course. They are passionate too about the mountain cheeses of their neighbours in the east, particularly Gruyère and Bleu de Bresse, which is a small and comparatively new blue cheese with a richness similar to that of a mountain Gorgonzola.

If you are travelling in the area, do look for the incredible range of local restaurant inns which specialize in regional dishes. They can be found in the tiny villages with names that are instantly recognizable from the wines that are grown on the slopes around them. If you are shopping, apart from the wines themselves there are marvellous mustards and cheeses to be bought, as well as a slice or two of *pain d'epice*, a honey-flavoured gingerbread. But perhaps the best advice is to stay in Burgundy as long as you can and revisit it soon. It is one of those places where nature has been so generous that nothing taken away tastes quite as good as it does when eaten on the spot.

Pâté de Campagne
COUNTRY PÂTÉ

This isn't of course confined to Burgundy, but the version they make there is particularly good. This is very simple to make, but it does need a food processor, otherwise you face serious work chopping and pounding and so on. Properly made, it should contain calf's liver, and the flavour does make it worth it, but unless the occasion is very special, use lamb's liver as it is a quarter of the price.

Put the bread into the food processor and turn it into breadcrumbs. Cut the onion into quarters and put that into the bowl and process for about 10 seconds until puréed. Take the purée out and put it to one side. Cut the liver and fat into 2.5cm/1 inch cubes and process these for 20 seconds. Add the thyme and oregano, a generous amount of salt and pepper and the eggs, and process until it is thoroughly mixed. Switch off, scrape down the sides and add the bread and onion purée. Process again until thoroughly mixed.

If you don't have a food processor, mince the breadcrumbs and onion, then the liver and fat. Put them all into a mixing bowl and add the herbs, seasonings and eggs and beat together thoroughly. This is not, I'm afraid, quite as easy as it sounds – you need a lot of effort to make the mixture really smooth!

Spoon the mixture into an oval terrine, smooth the top and decorate with bay leaves. Put the terrine into a baking tin, pour in enough water to come about 2.5cm/1 inch up the outside of the terrine, and put the whole lot into a medium oven at 180°C/160°C fan/350°F/Gas Mark 4, or the bottom of an Aga roasting oven, for 1–1¼ hours. Cover the pâté if necessary with a piece of foil. Check the level of the water occasionally. It has cooked when the pâté has shrunk away from the sides of the terrine a little.

Take the pâté out and allow it to cool for at least 12 hours, weighted down with a plate and a couple of heavy cans of baked beans or peas or whatever you happen to have in the larder on top, so the weight just presses the air out of it. When it is cool, you can either spoon it out and serve it, as they do in Burgundy, with moutarde à l'ancienne – that lovely mustard with grains in – and some gherkins, or you can tip it out of the terrine and slice it elegantly and serve it with a little salad. It will keep in the fridge, wrapped in clingfilm, for a week.

50g/2oz fresh white crustless bread

1 large onion

450g/1lb calf's or lamb's liver

100g/4oz chicken or goose fat, or the fat you find round beef kidneys

1 teaspoon dried thyme

1 teaspoon dried oregano

Salt and freshly ground black pepper

2 eggs

2 bay leaves

Soufflé au Fromage
CHEESE SOUFFLÉ

Serves 4

3 eggs, separated

3–4 tablespoons strong cheese, grated

Salt and freshly ground black pepper

For the Béchamel sauce:

300ml/10fl oz milk

1 heaped tablespoon cornflour

1 tablespoon butter

The perfect soufflé should be crisp and firm on the outside, with just a slight soft moistness at the centre. If you follow the recipe carefully, your soufflé too will be a confection of air surrounded by egg and rich with cheese. The cheese needs to be strong. A combination of Gruyère and Parmesan is marvellous, or just one or the other. Mature Cheddar is also suitable. A long time ago I was told to use cornflour, not plain flour in making the Béchamel sauce, and it really does make all the difference. Do practise though, before you go public!

To make the Béchamel sauce, whisk together in a saucepan the milk, cornflour and butter, and continue to whisk as it comes gently to the boil. When the sauce has thickened and is smooth, let it cool, then stir in the egg yolks. Beat the whites separately until absolutely stiff. Stir the cheese into the sauce, season, then fold in the beaten egg whites as lightly as you can so you don't force out too much air. Pour the mixture into a buttered 600ml/1 pint soufflé dish. Put the dish into a hot oven at 220°–230°C/190°–210°C fan/425°–450°F/Gas Mark 7–8, or the top of an Aga roasting oven, for 15–20 minutes, until the soufflé has risen and is golden on the top. You can sprinkle the top with some Parmesan or a very little coarse salt.

Truite Meunière
TROUT MEUNIÈRE

Burgundy is criss-crossed by a network of rivers, many of them teeming with trout. The French have also gone in for fish-farming in a big way. Their farmed trout are not pink like ours, they are still white – the difference is in what the trout are fed. Meunière actually means miller's wife, or mistress of the mill. Fish cooked this way are first lightly coated in flour. They are then fried in butter.

To coat the trout with the flour, you can mix together the flour and all the spices, put it on a plate and dip the trout in the mixture. The Crafty way, though, is to pour the flour, bay leaves, paprika, salt and pepper into a large plastic bag – a freezer bag is ideal – put in each fish in turn and shake the bag well – remembering to hold it tightly closed – until the fish is thoroughly coated.

In a large pan into which all the trout will fit, heat half the butter in the oil. Fry the trout quite briskly, but not so fast that they burn, for about 4–5 minutes on each side, depending on their size. To test when they are done, stick a fork very gently into the back, right by a fin. If the fish flakes, it's done, otherwise give it a minute longer. When they are completely cooked, put the fish on to warmed plates and wipe out the frying pan with a bit of kitchen paper – don't wash it. Melt the rest of the butter in the pan, and as soon as it stops sizzling, add the lemon juice. Stir it quickly, pour it over the trout, sprinkle with some chopped fresh parsley and serve at once. It needs nothing but some plain boiled potatoes.

Serves 4

4 trout, about 175g/6oz each

50g/2oz flour

½ teaspoon ground bay leaves

½ teaspoon paprika

½ teaspoon salt

½ teaspoon black pepper

50g/2oz butter, preferably unsalted

2 tablespoons oil

Juice of 1 lemon

Some chopped fresh parsley

Poulet à l'Ancienne
CHICKEN IN MUSTARD SAUCE

Serves 4

1 tablespoon oil

25g/1oz butter

4 boneless chicken breasts

250ml/8fl oz water

1 teaspoon cornflour

150ml/5fl oz single cream

2 tablespoons moutarde a l'ancienne

L'ancienne is what the whole-grain old-fashioned mustard is called, the kind that is sold in big pottery jars. It has a lovely pungent flavour, and although it doesn't have the eye-stinging quality of English mustard, it is definitely not mild! These days you can also buy it in smaller quantities in glass jars; the flavour is just as strong.

In a large frying pan, heat the butter in the oil. Put in the chicken breasts and sauté them, skin side down, for 3 minutes. Don't be tempted to add more fat: the skin contains fat and that comes out as the skin browns. Turn them over and sauté for another 5–6 minutes. Pour in the water and simmer gently for another 12–15 minutes until the chicken is cooked through. When they're done, put the chicken breasts on to warm plates. Mix the cornflour into the single cream, and pour the cream and mustard into the pan. Stir and bring it to the boil. The mustard helps to thicken the sauce as well as the cornflour, and the sauce turns a wonderful golden colour, with bite and crunch from the mustard grains. Pour it all over the chicken and serve at once.

HOW TO MAKE GOUGÈRE (CHEESY YORKSHIRE PUDDING)

Serves 4

75g/3oz plain flour

2 eggs

Pinch of salt

250ml/8fl oz milk, preferably full cream milk

4 tablespoons oil (not olive)

225g/8oz Gruyère or Cantal cheese

Gougères are served in Burgundy either hot or cold – and they are often offered during wine-tastings in the wonderful *caves* of the region. Here they are perfect for people who are partial to Yorkshire pudding, or like something to finish the Burgundy with – or both! I was taught to make these cheesy Yorkshire puddings by Fanny Craddock a long time ago, and they've been a great favourite ever since. The best cheese to use is either Gruyère or Cantal, which comes from just south-west of

Burgundy. You can use Lancashire or an old, mature Cheddar, but the flavour is very different and they don't melt in quite the same way.

Method:
In a large bowl, whisk the eggs, flour, milk and salt together. Then whisk in half the oil and leave the batter to stand for 30 minutes. Cut the cheese into small cubes (about 5mm/¼ inch) and stir these into the batter. Put the remaining 2 tablespoons of oil into a baking dish and heat it in the oven until it

sizzles. Pour the batter into the sizzling oil and bake it in a hot oven at 200°C/180°C fan/400°F/Gas Mark 6, or the top of an Aga roasting oven, for 35–40 minutes, until the batter has risen and turned golden, and the cheese has melted into it.

Filet Rôti
FILLET OF BEEF

Fillet of beef is quite simply the most luxurious roast beef ever! At a price it can be found in the top restaurants, where it is often so tender it is, as they say, like butter. Fillet *is* very expensive to buy, but it is a splendid treat. Cooked with care, yours too will be as tender as butter and with a marvellous flavour. Ask your butcher to tie the fillet for roasting and to make sure it is about 45cm/18 inches long and an even thickness along its length.

Heat a frying pan large enough for the fillet until it is very hot. Add the oil, then immediately roll the fillet in it for 2–3 minutes until all sides are brown. Take the meat out of the frying pan and put it on a rack in a roasting tin. Spread it with the butter, season generously with salt and pepper, and roast in a hot oven at 230°C/210°C fan/450°F/Gas Mark 8, or use the top of an Aga roasting oven, for 22 minutes per kg/10 minutes per lb. At the end of the cooking time, take the beef out of the oven and allow it to rest in a warm place for 5–10 minutes while you deglaze the juices in the roasting tin with your chosen liquid – beef stock, cranberry juice or red wine. Put the roasting tin on the stove and bring the mixture quickly to the boil until it has reduced to about 120ml/4fl oz of the most delicious gravy. Serve the beef cut across the grain in slices about 1cm/½ inch thick. They should still be pink in the middle. Courgettes, crisp green beans and Pommes Dauphinois (see p. 152) go marvellously with this.

Serves 4–6

3 tablespoons oil

1.5kg/3lb beef fillet

50g/2oz butter

Salt and freshly ground black pepper

250ml/8fl oz beef stock, cranberry juice or red wine

Forester's Pheasant
(page 110)
Pears in Red Wine
(page 111)

Faisan Forestière
FORESTER'S PHEASANT

Serves 4

1 large pheasant, jointed

25g/1oz butter

1 tablespoon oil

1 large onion, peeled and finely chopped

4 sticks celery, cut in 1cm/½ inch slices

225g/8oz carrots, cut into 5 × 1cm/2 × ½ inch batons

4 tablespoons red wine vinegar

Salt and freshly ground black pepper

300ml/10fl oz red grape juice

Bouquet garni of 1 stick celery, 1 bay leaf, a sprig of thyme, 4 sprigs parsley, or use a shop-bought sachet

10 pickling onions, peeled

225g/8oz mushrooms: ceps or morels if you can get them, otherwise chestnut or oyster mushrooms

2 teaspoons arrowroot or potato flour

Chopped fresh parsley

Plump pheasants and intensely flavoured mushrooms make a marvellous combination. Pheasants are readily available in season from supermarkets as well as from specialist game-dealers. In Burgundy, the liquid used would, of course, be a red Burgundy, but I prefer the lighter taste of red grape juice.

In an ovenproof casserole, heat the butter in the oil and brown the pieces of pheasant over a high heat. Add the onion, celery and carrots and turn them in the juices. Pour in the wine vinegar, bring to the boil, and allow it almost to boil away. Season generously with salt and pepper, and add the grape juice and bouquet garni. Bring back to the boil, cover, and simmer gently for 25 minutes.

The easiest way to peel pickling onions is to put them into a bowl of boiling water. Leave them for about 30 seconds and their skins should then slip off easily. If the mushrooms are large, cut them into walnut-sized pieces. Put the onions and mushrooms into the casserole, then put the dish into a medium oven at 180°C/160°C fan/350°F/Gas Mark 4, or the bottom of an Aga roasting oven, for 20 minutes.

To serve, mix the arrowroot or potato flour into a little water to make a smooth paste, and stir it into the casserole which you have again taken out of the oven. Put the casserole back on top of the stove, and heat to boiling point until the sauce thickens and clears. Serve sprinkled with chopped parsley. There are plenty of vegetables in the casserole, but Celeriac and Potato Purée (see p. 151) also goes very well with this.

Poires au Vin Rouge
PEARS IN RED WINE

Serves 6

6 firm pears

175–225g/6–8oz sugar

1 teaspoon ground allspice

2 teaspoons ground ginger

450ml/15fl oz red wine, red grape juice or cranberry juice

Burgundy excels in just about all its food and wine products, and fruit is no exception. It is used for pies and tarts, fruit-based confectionery, and as here, where the quality of the individual fruits is all important. The pears need to be firm but ripe and you need large ones. You can use either Comice or Conference pears. The amount of sugar you use depends on how sweet the pears are, and how sweet your tooth is. If you have the time to cook this really slowly, your patience will be well-rewarded!

Peel the pears, leaving on the stalks, and take the core out. Lay them in an ovenproof dish and sprinkle with the sugar, allspice and ginger. Half-cover with the wine or juice, and top up with just enough water to cover the pears. Bake in a very low oven at 120°C/110°C fan/250°F/Gas Mark ½, for between 5 and 7 hours, turning the pears a couple of times. If you have an Aga, put them in the simmering oven and leave overnight. They will deepen to a mahogany colour and the wine or juice will reduce to a rich syrup.

If you need to cook them more quickly, you can cook them on top of the stove. Poach the pears very, very gently in a saucepan for 1½ hours. Remove them from the saucepan with a slotted spoon and rapidly boil the liquid until it has reduced to a syrup. Pour over the pears and allow to cool.

Serve in a shallow bowl, with the pears piled up in a pyramid, with the stalks uppermost. A little cream looks and tastes good with this.

BURGUNDY CHEESEBOARD

Burgundy is one of the most beautiful regions of France and produces food and wine hard to beat anywhere. The cheeses made here are marvellous – many of them strong with a powerful aroma. They are often flavoured with herbs such as thyme, bay or tarragon, washed in white wine or stored in *marc*. Unhappily you have to hunt in this country for them and you may have to substitute full-flavoured cheeses from elsewhere in France for your Burgundy cheeseboard.

Époisses *is* sold here in specialist shops. It is a marvellous cows' milk cheese, made throughout Burgundy. The deep-orange crust is washed with sage, then with a Burgundy *marc*. The result is a deep, intense, fruity flavour, one of the great cheeses of France.

Soumaintrain is also a cows' milk cheese, but you are unlikely to find it in this country. It has a pronounced smell and spicy flavour, with a washed reddish-brown rind. It is a seasonal cheese, at its best from spring to autumn. Like most of the Burgundy cheeses it is marvellous with a full-bodied Burgundy, my wine-drinking friends tell me.

Saint Florentin is also made from cows' milk. It is a soft, quite strongly flavoured cheese when it is ripe, with a washed edible rind. It is also sold – though alas, not in Britain – when it is young, when it has a sweet, mild, milky flavour.

BRITTANY

Brittany, or little Britain as the name implies, was – according to local folklore – settled by Celts fleeing from the Anglo-Saxon invasion after the collapse of Rome in the fifth century. This theory is supported by the fact that Welsh-speaking people and those Bretons who still speak their own language understand one another. Brittany is the part of France that sticks out into the Atlantic, with the great dog's head of Brest on the end of it forming the westernmost point of the whole of mainland France. Surrounded by the sea on three sides, Brittany has a mild but damp climate. It is far enough south for the sun to ameliorate some of the worst effects of the weather of northern Europe, and while it is not frost free it is a marvellous place for growing fruit and vegetables. Running inland from the Breton coast along the northern bank of the Loire are the ancient provinces of Maine, Angou and Touraine, up until the late Middle Ages ruled directly by English kings. It is here that the promise of Brittany's richness reaches its fruition in the region's pasturelands, orchards and fields.

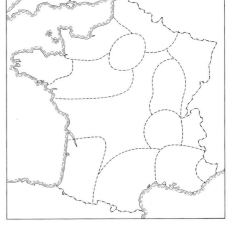

Until as recently as the middle of the nineteenth century Brittany was regarded by the rest of France as fairly primitive. Transport was difficult, except by sea, and as a result the Bretons never developed the sophisticated tastes and cooking that the rest of France took for granted. Perhaps the greatest example of this is the Breton pancake which, paradoxically, has swept back during the twentieth century to conquer cafés and street corners across the whole of France. Originally pancakes were the poor person's alternative – sometimes the only alternative – to bread, representing an easy-to-cook form of flour-based nourishment which didn't require the sophistication of baking ovens. They are often made from buckwheat, a coarse grain which makes a thick and substantial pancake that is almost always eaten as a savoury. There are also wheaten pancakes in southern Brittany, and famous crêpes known as *dentelles*, frilly pancakes made with such fine and thin batter that they turn into edible lace as they cook. Even these beautiful pancakes were seen as a sign of poverty until recently, but they have now won over the rest of the world with their sheer deliciousness.

The sea dominates in Brittany, with shellfish, mussels, lobster, clams and shrimp all playing their part. One of the most famous dishes of all is lobster *sauce amoricaine*, named not – as you might

Opposite: The tiny fishing village of Erquy, which is celebrated for its scallops.

think – for the United States but for the old name of Brittany, Amorique. To accompany the shellfish and the river fish is the famous *beurre blanc* sauce. Made from shallots and a lightly salted butter, it is widely held to be the greatest of all sauces to serve with fish. Fish stews are famous in Brittany, too, none more so than *cotriade*. This is the northern equivalent of *bouillabaisse*, a fisherman's stew originally made with the fish that was left over from market; like *bouillabaisse*, this stew has become a hugely fashionable and popular dish.

Meat is of an excellent quality in Brittany, in particular *agneau pré-salé*, or salt meadow lamb, which has become well known throughout France. These days much of the lamb eaten in the region comes from Britain, brought across the water from the salt marshes of Romney and the Medway where similar conditions exist. Cattle, too, flourish in Brittany, and the area specializes in a range of dishes based on offal, not the least of which is a kind of tripe sausage called *andouillettes*.

Unlike the Mediterranean region, Brittany still offers an authentic style of cooking in its numerous restaurants and harbour cafés. This is partly because the North Atlantic has not yet been over-fished in the way that the Mediterranean has. The coastline itself is very varied and ranges from high and forbidding cliffs to great shallow tidal bays like Morbihan, with their tiny rock-strewn anchorages and great sweeping areas of drying sand and mud. This dominant coastline means that Brittany is becoming an increasingly popular holiday destination, but it still retains – perhaps more than any other part of western France – a sense of its own identity and independence. There is a strong separatist movement in Brittany, based not least on a more 'green' approach to life, which is much more defined than the policies of central government.

When you are visiting Brittany, be sure to pursue the truly local food of the region. Try the *plats de fruits de mer* which comprise the most sumptuous array of shellfish, from the tiniest winkles to whole crabs and lobsters. Usually this dish is served with a great bowl of mayonnaise, made milder than the fruity olive oil dips of the South. Oysters are served raw and cooked, and fish everywhere in the region can be eaten either simply poached or grilled with the famous *beurre blanc*. Try too some of the wonderful vegetables of the area: the quality of the carrots, leeks, tiny purple-skinned turnips and a profusion of salad vegetables, is superb. The ubiquitous Brittany Ferries actually grew out of a network of vegetable suppliers who started their own shipping line to transport artichokes and other special garden produce to Britain.

There are really no special cheeses in Brittany, although the *crémettes*, fresh cream cheeses often eaten as a dessert with fresh fruit or fruit conserves, are a speciality of the region, and Breton butter rivals that of neighbouring Normandy as one of the best in France. It is a salted butter, unlike that of Normandy, and much favoured for cooking as well as spreading.

The north of Brittany shares the northern European taste for cider rather than wine, but down near the Loire there are vineyards stretching for miles, and the wines that grow there – almost all of them white – are excellent for complementing fish dishes. Finally, if you are in the south of Brittany near the great port of Nantes, do try the duck with green peas. If you thought duck was meant to be a British dish, you are in for one of the most pleasant culinary surprises I know

Les Artichauts
ARTICHOKES

Artichokes thrive in Brittany; in fact after cauliflowers they are one of the biggest exports from there. They look like giant thistles, which is just what they are. There are 3 classic ways of serving them: hot with melted butter, or with Hollandaise Sauce (see p. 118), or cold with a Vinaigrette (see p. 26). Once you have cooked them, the choice is yours.

Trim the stalks off each artichoke parallel with the base, and cook in plenty of boiling water with a tablespoon of wine vinegar for 25–30 minutes. To eat them, which you do with your fingers, simply peel off each leaf and dip it into melted butter or Hollandaise sauce if they are hot, or vinaigrette if cold. When you get to the hairy bit in the middle, scoop it out and discard. You are now left with what many people think is the best bit, the base or heart, which is deliciously edible.

Serves 1 artichoke per person

1 artichoke per person

1 tablespoon wine vinegar

Choufleur Vinaigrette
CAULIFLOWER VINAIGRETTE

Brittany produces vast quantities of cauliflowers; indeed, Brittany Ferries, which now takes people on holiday, was originally set up to export the cauliflowers and artichokes from Brittany to Britain. This is a cauliflower salad. The quantities given for the dressing will make more than you actually need for this, but the rest will keep happily in the fridge.

Bring a large saucepan of salted water to the boil. While this is happening, make the dressing. You can make it in a screw-top jar, in a food processor or in a bowl with a

Serves 4

1 cauliflower

2 tablespoons each chopped fresh chives and parsley

For the vinaigrette:

2 tablespoons fresh
lemon juice

2 tablespoons cider or
white wine vinegar

1 teaspoon caster sugar

½ teaspoon salt

2 tablespoons olive oil

250ml/8fl oz sunflower
or salad oil

whisk. First mix together the lemon juice, vinegar, sugar and salt until the salt and sugar are thoroughly dissolved. Don't add the oil until this has happened. Then add the olive oil and sunflower oil and either give it a thorough shake or whizz it in the food processor. Wash and trim the cauliflower and put it in the pan of boiling water. Boil it for 6–8 minutes until the stem is just tender.

Take out the cauliflower and plunge it into cold water to stop it cooking. Break it into big chunks, 4–6 pieces is about right. Take it out of the water and, drain it and, while it is still a little warm, pour half the vinaigrette over it. Leave it for at least 30 minutes to soak up all the juices. Turn it over just before serving, spoon the vinaigrette that has run off it back over the top, and sprinkle the cauliflower with the fresh chives and parsley. This is a marvellous, substantial starter.

Cotriade
BRETON FISH STEW

Serves 4

900g/2lb filleted fish

2 large onions, peeled
and chopped

900g/2lb potatoes,
peeled and chopped, a
salad variety is best for
this

Generous handful fresh
parsley

**To make the fish
stock:**

2 bay leaves

Juice of 1 lemon

Salt and freshly ground
black pepper

1 large sprig thyme

Parsley stalks

1 stick celery

Optional:

2 tablespoons single
cream

1 teaspoon fresh lemon
juice

1 teaspoon cornflour

Cotriade, a combined soup and stew, is the great fish dish of Brittany, in the way that Bouillabaisse (see p. 168) and Bourride (see p. 42) are the great fish dishes of the Mediterranean. Like all fishermen's stews, it is made by and large from whatever you happen to have to hand. The 3 constant ingredients are fish, potatoes and parsley. The type of fish really does depend on what is available. You can use any combination of cod, mackerel, haddock, whiting, monkfish, bass, gurnet or coley and you can add shellfish if you like.

Put all the ingredients for the stock into a big saucepan with 1.75l/3 pints/7½ cups of water. Bring to the boil and simmer for 30–40 minutes. Strain it, and into the liquid put the potatoes and onions. Bring to the boil and simmer until the potatoes are almost cooked, about 10–12 minutes. Cut the fish into cubes or neat pieces and put these into the saucepan. If you are using shellfish, such as raw prawns or mussels or cockles, add them too. When the fish is just cooked – it will take about 4–5 minutes – turn off the heat and stir in the parsley. The stew is now ready to eat. If you want to add the cream, stir the lemon juice into it and add the cornflour. Mix it together, then stir it into the cotriade. It just adds a little creamy smoothness to the sauce. It isn't traditional, but I like it!

In Brittany they serve cotriade in 2 ways. You either eat the whole thing in an enormous bowl, or you take the liquid off first and eat that as a soup, and then have the potatoes and fish as a main course.

Gigot Pré-Salé
BRETON ROAST LAMB

Pré-salé is not a restaurant or a famous chef; it actually translates as 'salt meadow'! So *gigot pré-salé* is actually a leg of lamb which comes from the salt meadows bordering the seashore in Brittany, where the lamb is meant to have the flavour of the herbs which it has eaten in the summer months. I think I take that story with a large pinch *de sel*, but this is none the less a lovely way to cook our own very good home-grown lamb. In fact, much of the pré-salé lamb sold in France comes not from Brittany, but from the Romney marshes on the Kent–Sussex border, where similar conditions exist – water meadows fed by the sea.

Crush the peeled garlic cloves with the sea salt and mix together with the oil. Spread this lovely garlicky, salty paste over the top of the lamb as if spreading butter. Place the lamb on a wire rack over a roasting tin into which you have poured the water and arrange the fresh rosemary round the sides of the lamb. Heat the oven to 190°C/170°C fan/375°F/Gas Mark 5, or use the middle of the Aga, and cook for 15 minutes per 500g/1lb plus 15 minutes for pink lamb, 20 minutes per 500g/1lb plus 20 minutes for a medium-done roast, and 25 minutes per 500g/1lb plus 25 minutes for frazzled!

When it is cooked, take it out of the oven and let it stand in a warm place for at least 10 minutes before carving. This relaxes the meat, so instead of being rubbery as it would be if you carved it immediately, it is butter-tender. You can cover it loosely with tin foil if you like. The water in the roasting tin will have reduced to about 150ml/5fl oz, and will have the flavour of lamb and herbs. You can thicken it with a little cornflour to make the most delicious gravy, or leave it just as it is. Serve with lots of freshly boiled potatoes only – a vegetable should come as another course as the flavours are too good to dilute.

Serves 6

1 leg of lamb, about 1.5-1.75kg/3½-4lb

2 cloves garlic, peeled

25g/1oz sea salt

1 tablespoon oil

600ml/1 pint water

2 large sprigs fresh rosemary

Sole au Beurre Blanc
SOLE IN WHITE BUTTER SAUCE

Serves 4

4 generous fillets of Dover or lemon sole, about 175–225g/6–8oz each

1 heaped teaspoon cornflour

175g/6oz unsalted butter

1 tablespoon chopped fresh parsley

For the court bouillon:

600ml/1 pint water

Bones and trimmings from the filleted fish

1 bay leaf

Sprig of parsley

Juice of 1 lemon

1 tablespoon white wine vinegar

1 teaspoon salt

6 peppercorns

Brittany produces some marvellous butter, as well as wonderfully fresh fish. You need unsalted butter for this recipe, but keep an eye out for the delicious Brittany butter with grains of sea salt in it. You can use either lemon sole or the more expensive Dover sole for this recipe. Many people are put off trying to cook beurre blanc as it has the reputation of being a chef's sauce and pretty tricky. This, however, is the Crafty Cook's method!

Make the court bouillon first. Put the water, fish trimmings, bay leaf, parsley, lemon juice, vinegar, salt and peppercorns into a large saucepan. Bring this to the boil and simmer for about 15 minutes. Butter a baking dish and put the fillets into it. Pour the court bouillon over the sole and bake in a medium oven at 180°C/160°C fan/350°F/Gas Mark 4, or the bottom of an Aga roasting oven, for 10–15 minutes until the sole just flakes. How long the fillets take to cook depends on how thick they are.

When they're done, take them out of the oven and keep warm. Strain the liquid and put 5 large tablespoons (or 150ml/5fl oz) into a saucepan. Slake the cornflour – stir the teaspoonful into a little of the liquid – then add it to the saucepan and stir it in. Chop the butter into 1cm/½ inch cubes and add to the pan. Whisk it over a medium heat until the butter melts and the sauce thickens slightly until it's the consistency of single cream and a lovely pale gold with the flavour of the herbs. Chefs don't add the cornflour, but its addition ensures that the beurre blanc doesn't separate, provided, that is, you don't boil it. If you do, it will become oily and separate even with the cornflour. Pour it over the sole and sprinkle with chopped fresh parsley. Serve with little green beans and plain freshly boiled potatoes.

HOW TO MAKE A SIMPLE HOLLANDAISE SAUCE

1 egg

1 egg yolk

Salt to taste

Juice of ½ lemon

175g/6oz butter, cubed

Egg emulsion sauces are notorious for being hard to make – curdling, separating and requiring lots of attention. This is a slightly lighter version than the more traditional Hollandaise and it is *not* difficult to prepare. You must, however, make this version in a liquidizer or food processor.

Method:
Pour the egg and the egg yolk into the machine and process until well mixed. Add a pinch of salt and the lemon juice and process for another 5–10 seconds until thoroughly blended. In a non-stick saucepan, heat the butter until it foams. At the moment it stops hissing, pour it into the processor through the feed tube, with the motor running. Allow it to process for 10 seconds after all the butter has been poured in. Tip the mixture back into the pan, but do not replace on the heat; there is enough heat in the pan to finish thickening the sauce, which can be kept warm for up to 10 minutes before serving.

Omelette Soufflée
SOUFFLÉ OMELETTE

Soufflé omelettes look spectacular, but they are really easy to make. They make a lovely lunch dish, or a very impressive end to a dinner party. Simply adjust the filling and topping accordingly.

For sweet omelette fillings: 1 tablespoon per person of a good French-style conserve or jam. You could also add a teaspoon of toasted, slivered almonds.

For savoury omelette fillings: 1 tablespoon of flaked, cooked smoked haddock mixed with cream, or white crab meat, or finely grated fresh Parmesan or Gruyère cheese.

Preheat the grill. Beat the egg yolks together. In a separate bowl, beat the egg whites until they are stiff, then fold them into the yolks. Heat a small frying pan, about 12–15cm/5–6 inches across, preferably non-stick, until it is very hot. Add the butter. As soon as it stops sizzling, pour in the omelette mixture and cook over a high heat. It will puff up and the bottom will set. Put the omelette in its pan under the grill for about 30 seconds to set the top. Spread the filling over half the omelette, fold over gently and sprinkle the top with the sugar or cheese. Serve immediately on a warm plate. It looks lovely and squashy, rather like a folded cushion, but happily tastes, not of cushion, but of wonderfully light egg and whatever filling you have chosen.

Per person:

2 eggs, separated

1 teaspoon butter

1 tablespoon appropriate filling

1 teaspoon icing sugar for a sweet omelette, or grated cheese for a savoury one

Crêpes Suzette
(page 122)

Crêpes Suzette

Serves 4

50g/2oz/½ stick butter

120ml/4fl oz fresh
orange juice

2 tablespoons orange
and lemon marmalade

Grated rind of 1 lemon

8 crêpes (opposite)

1–2 tablespoons brandy
or rum (optional)

Crêpes Suzette is the sort of grand and complicated dish that the more traditional restaurants love to show off. It requires grating the rinds of oranges and lemons using lump sugar and flambéing the crêpes in front of impressed diners. The result is delicious, but far too involved to make at home. This method demands none of that, but none the less results in Crêpes Suzette pretty well indistinguishable from the more elaborate version.

In a large frying pan, about 30cm/12 inches across, melt the butter until it foams. Add the orange juice and the marmalade and stir gently until the mixture melts together. Sprinkle on the grated lemon rind, and then add the crêpes, one by one, making sure they are coated in the sauce. Fold them into quarters and pile them on one side of the pan as you finish each one. You should be able to get 8 pancakes into a 30cm/12 inch pan using this method.

If you are feeling brave, you can at this point flambé the crêpes with 1–2 tablespoons of brandy or rum, making sure all the alcohol is burned off before you serve the dish or it will taste awful. If you don't want the pyrotechnics, serve the pancakes hot, straight out of the pan on to warm plates, 2 per person, with a good spoonful of the sauce that should still be swimming around in the bottom of the pan.

BRITTANY CHEESEBOARD

The meadows of Brittany produce rich, creamy cows' milk cheeses, the most famous of which are widely available here. To complete your Brittany cheeseboard, you may need to choose a blue cheese and a goats' cheese from elsewhere in France for proper balance.

Port Salut is a familiar sight in supermarkets here, though the quality can vary quite a lot. The washed crust is a deep yellow, the cheese, made from cows' milk, varies from a pale, bland colour and taste to a rich deep gold with a marvellous fruity flavour, depending on age. The cheese was created by Trappist monks in their abbey at Entrammes, which they named Port-du-Salut, Haven of Safety.

St Paulin is a derivative of Port Salut, also readily available in this country. It is now made all over France. The taste is quite sweet and the texture semi-soft and smooth.

HOW TO MAKE CRÊPES (FRENCH PANCAKES)

Brittany claims to be the natural home of the crêpe, and all over France crêperies advertise the fact that they are the real Breton thing. Basic crêpes are dead easy to make. You can make them with plain (all-purpose) flour, or replace 1 tablespoon of the plain flour with 1 tablespoon of wholemeal flour. That adds a lovely texture, particularly if you are eating these as savoury crêpes. Do not make the whole thing with wholemeal flour, you will end up with shoe leather! You have a great choice as to what liquid to use: the French use orange juice for sweet pancakes, beer for savoury ones, or just ordinary water. In Britain we tend to use half milk and half water. The main points to remember are that the frying pan must be big, solid and flat, that the crêpes are meant to be so thin you can almost see through them, that the batter must be absolutely smooth and that you must let it stand for at least

30 minutes before making the crêpes.

Method:
Put all the ingredients into a food processor or liquidizer or basin and whizz it or beat it until it is blended, lump-free and absolutely smooth. Then let it stand for at least 30 minutes in the fridge. Up to an hour and a half won't hurt it. Letting it stand is important as a chemical change takes place in the flour letting it expand and absorb the liquid and making it far easier to handle.

Heat a large, solid, flat and preferably non-stick frying pan (a 25cm/10 inch pan is ideal), and pour a little oil into it. Swirl the oil round, then get rid of it – pour it into a bowl, or carefully wipe it out with a bit of kitchen paper – remember the pan is very hot! Also remember, the first pancake never works, so if it comes to pieces, do not despair. Pour in enough mixture – about 1 tablespoon – to make a

puddle in the middle of the pan and tilt the pan so it runs round the edges. There should be just enough to cover the bottom of the pan. If there is too much, just pour it back into the jug or basin. The batter will set and the edges will curl. It may be so thin that there are even a few holes in it where the bubbles have burst, but don't panic! Let it set for 30–45 seconds, then gently ease up the edges with a spatula or fish slice and turn the crêpe over. Cook for another 30 seconds, then put it on a warm plate.

Either serve the crêpes as you cook them, or put some greaseproof paper over the top and continue making the pancakes until you have a stack. Every 2 or 3 pancakes, you will need to re-oil the pan. Serve them with a little icing sugar and lemon juice, apricot jam, or even hot chocolate sauce and whipped cream! If you're serving them as a savoury, a little spinach and grated cheese is delicious.

Serves 4

100g/4oz plain flour

2 eggs, beaten

1 tablespoon oil

Pinch of salt

300ml/10fl oz orange juice, beer, or water

oil for frying

LOIRE

Ihave a particular fondness for the Loire region. On my first adult trip to France, I arrived on the banks of the Loire at Orléans, after three days' hard travelling. It proved the perfect place for a memorable cooling dip. Although Orléans is over 100 miles from the sea, the river at this point is over 150 yards wide. It rises south of Lyon, far away on the edge of the Alps, and reaches the sea on the border of Brittany at Nantes, on the Atlantic coast. Along all its length the Loire runs through some of the most peaceful and gentle countryside in France. One of France's greatest gastronomes, Curnonsky, described the region as the centre of *la mesure*, moderation. The inhabitants seem to be more at peace with themselves than in other, more frenetic parts of this industrious country, and even the climate is a moderate one, falling between the cold winters of northern Europe and the bitingly hot summers of the South.

Orléans itself is a much quieter city than it was when Joan of Arc made her reputation by lifting the British siege of the town. Despite the town's exciting history, the surrounding area is one where the French have indulged their fantasies, as the great châteaux along the river so clearly attest. These are a tourist attraction now, but during the French Renaissance – around the time that Henry VIII and Elizabeth I occupied the English throne – the valley of the Loire was a theatre in which the great nobles of France competed to show off their wealth. Such extravagances brought many of them to catastrophe, but fortunately most of the castles that beggared them have survived for our enjoyment. They make a wonderful excuse for touring gently through some of the most beautiful countryside in France and enjoying the delicious produce on offer.

The Loire itself supplies a great deal of this produce, with river fish like carp and eels, pike and chad served as local specialities. River fish can be bony and are occasionally quite dry, so a range of rich sauces, many of them based on butter flavoured with little more than shallots and vinegar, has developed to accompany them. Quantities of Atlantic salmon also swim up the Loire and are caught there every year. Around the great coastal port of Nantes, with its enormous bridge over the mouth of the Loire, sea fish and shellfish reign. I remember an amazing hors d'oeuvre which appeared as if out of a fairytale: the

Opposite: The Lac du Grand Lieu, a remote, reed-fringed lake in the Loire Atlantique.

grandfather of the family we were staying with went off with a net and came back with a pailful of local shrimp that he had caught while standing breast-high in the tide. We ate them with fresh bread and wonderful local butter, accompanied by radishes from the garden and tiny Cos lettuces broken into leaves. Against the backdrop of the beach and a sun-kissed Atlantic, it made the most delicious first course. Hors d'oeuvres like this one lie at the very heart of good cooking in the Loire, making the most of home-grown produce with an emphasis on the balance of texture with an intensity of flavour.

Further inland the orchards enjoy pride of place. Apples are a speciality of the region, particularly the famous *reinettes* – close in style, flavour and texture to our own Cox's. Plums, apricots and peaches also grow in abundance, and the prunes from around Tours are famous throughout the world. The area specializes too in *primeurs*, baby vegetables that have become the gourmet's delight. Some, like carrots and turnips, can be found elsewhere, but others – asparagus and baby artichokes – are less common. Artichokes are normally prepared as simply as possible, blanched and then cooked for the last moment or two in lightly seasoned butter. Garlic is famous in this region, too, and for centuries Tours has held a garlic and basil festival each July, highlighting the great value placed on the herbs and flavourings grown in the Loire valley area.

The Loire does have some charcuterie, but the poultry of the region is outstanding. Chickens from around Le Mans are almost as famous as those of their rivals in Bresse, and chicken dishes abound throughout the province; and Nantes is celebrated for its duck, which is cooked both in the traditional way – with the breast roasted and the legs grilled in order to achieve a contrast in textures while cooking the whole bird *au point* – and in various sautés, casseroles and a famous galantine or jelly-set pâté.

When you come to the last courses of the meal the Loire also holds its head high: its cheeses include *bâtons* – sticks of goats' cheese from the area around St Maure – and fresh cream cheeses called *crémettes* which are soft, white and very mild in flavour. These are delicious when eaten with soft fresh fruits. A combination of cheese and strawberries is the local equivalent to our strawberries and cream, usually eaten with a light sifting of caster sugar. Sometimes the *crémettes* are arranged in specially-shaped moulds, either in perfect rounds or in hearts – in which case they become *coeurs à la crème*. Fruits have pride of place in the puddings of the Loire, and even in the pâtisseries it is the strawberry and almond tarts that are the best choices. Although no one is quite sure where *crème pâtissière*, confectioner's custard, originated, it is certainly very much in evidence in the tarts of this region.

British people tend to find the food of the Loire most *convenable* to the English palate. As the Loire is a tourist trap, particularly in the summer, it is worth looking for small restaurants and inns slightly off the beaten track. In the hotels and restaurants that cluster around the great châteaux one can suffer quite easily from the casually cooked food and even more casual service that mass tourism always seems to produce. Tourism also tends to push up the prices of the celebrated wines of the region, particularly the wines designed to accompany fish like Sancerre, Pouilly and Vouvray. Wines are nevertheless a favourite purchase to bring back to England, as are some of the more portable vegetables. If you are passing through at the right time of year, do buy some of the wonderfully fat and tender mauve asparagus and some of the butter from the area around Préfailles. This combination makes one of the most delicious and simple dishes I know.

HOW TO ASSEMBLE HORS D'OEUVRE

I have this wonderful memory of a lunch one summer with French friends, sitting on a beach at the mouth of the Loire, right on the Atlantic. The grandfather of the family had gone fishing for little pink shrimps which we ate as a starter with some radishes, bread and butter, and it was just one of those perfect days – almost like a French painting! Hors d'oeuvre literally means something outside the main business, something you eat before you get down to the serious business of the main course. A good hors d'oeuvre, however, can be quite substantial in its own right. It should contain just 4–6 items and the Crafty trick is to buy these – not to make them!

For a basic 4-dish hors d'oeuvre, you need a contrasting combination of textures and flavours, so 1 dish should be fishy, 1 meaty, 1 made of vegetables and 1 sharp and spicy.

Let's start with fish. Supermarkets and speciality shops are full of all kinds of preserved and pickled fish. You could choose from sardines, smoked salmon, mackerel au vin blanc or smoked oysters. All you have to do is open the packet or the can! In Paris, the great food shop Fauchon sells canned sardines so special and expensive that you are supposed to lay them down for 5 years, turning them every 6 months! More realistically, you can buy very good sardines in olive oil in most supermarkets here.

In contrast, the vegetable dish should be raw. The French call them crudités. You could include a grated carrot mayonnaise, celeriac remoulade, celery and walnuts, fresh radishes or a tomato and anchovy salad. Don't do all of these – just 1 or 2 (see recipe ideas, below).

The meat dish again depends on your taste. There are literally hundreds of different salamis to choose from – buy them thinly sliced. Or you could choose smoked sausage, wafer-thin turkey breast, pâté, or cold beef in a vinaigrette.

Before you decide on a sharp and spicy dish, make sure there is nothing too sharp and spicy in the meat or fish dishes you have chosen, or nothing that would clash with, say, olives, gherkins, capers or pickled mushrooms, pickled peperonata and so on.

With all of these, you need some good French bread and unsalted butter.

Vegetable recipes
GRATED CARROT
MAYONNAISE
Peel and grate some carrots and stir into them some mayonnaise, with a little chopped spring onion.

CELERIAC
REMOULADE
Peel the celeriac and grate it. Add a teaspoon of mustard to some mayonnaise, and mix it all together.

TOMATO AND
ANCHOVY SALAD
Slice a couple of big, juicy tomatoes very thinly, sprinkle with some finely chopped spring onions (scallions), and top with a few anchovy fillets and Vinaigrette dressing (p. 26).

Potage aux Champignons
MUSHROOM SOUP

Serves 4

450g/1lb wild mushrooms or 350g/12oz chestnut or flat mushrooms, preferably organic

25g/1oz dried mushrooms

50g/2oz butter

1 onion, peeled and chopped

900ml/1½ pints chicken stock or 600ml/1 pint chicken stock and 300ml/10fl oz of the mushroom soaking liquid (see method)

2 slices white bread, crusts removed

Salt and freshly ground black pepper

150ml/5fl oz single cream

Mushroom soup made from wild mushrooms has the most extraordinarily intense flavour. Imagine foraging through the woods of the Loire at daybreak, gathering armfuls of dew-covered mushrooms! It is a wonderfully romantic notion, but it can be lethal unless you are an expert on how to tell an edible mushroom from a toadstool. You can, however, approach the wonderful flavour by adding dried mushrooms to good, full-flavoured cultivated ones, such as organic chestnut or field mushrooms.

Soak the dried mushrooms in boiling water for 15 minutes. Drain and reserve the liquid. Trim the fresh mushrooms and put them into a colander. Pour a kettle of boiling water over them to clean them. Don't peel. Slice all the mushrooms neatly. Melt the butter in a large pan and cook the onion and mushrooms over a medium heat for 5 minutes. Add the chicken stock, or chicken stock and mushroom liquid, and simmer, covered, for 20 minutes. Crumble the bread into the soup. Add the seasoning, and liquidize or purée the mushrooms through a sieve. Pour the soup back into the saucepan, add the cream and reheat gently – don't let it boil. Serve with croûtons.

Salade de Coquilles St Jacques aux Asperges
SALAD OF SCALLOPS AND ASPARAGUS

Serves 4

4 large scallops, shelled

225g/8oz asparagus

50g/2oz pine nuts

2 tablespoons olive oil

1 frilly-leafed lettuce or 1 chicory

Salt and freshly ground black pepper

The scallops from this region are superb – big and plump with a wonderfully delicate flavour. The combination of textures and flavours in this very luxurious salad is a revelation – and it also looks very pretty.

Remove the coral half-moons from the scallops and put them on one side. Cut each scallop across the grain into 3 slices. Trim and wash the asparagus, and steam in a steamer if you have one or a colander over boiling water for 9 minutes. In a frying pan, fry the pine nuts in the olive oil for 2 minutes, making sure they don't burn but just turn golden. Remove the pine nuts, but keep the oil in the frying pan. Fill 4 of your most elegant serving bowls with washed and drained lettuce or chicory, torn into pieces about the size of half a postcard. Let the asparagus cool a little, then lay them on the lettuce and sprinkle the pine nuts over the top.

Mix the dressing ingredients together in a liquidizer or pour them all into a screw-top jar and shake vigorously. Reheat the oil that the pine nuts were cooked in until it is very hot, and add the slices of scallop. Cook for 1 minute on each side, add the coral half-moons, season with a little salt and pepper, and cook for 1 more minute. Place the scallops on the lettuce or endive and pour 2 tablespoons of dressing over each bowl. Serve while still warm.

For the dressing:

6 tablespoons salad oil

1 teaspoon sugar

1 teaspoon salt

1 tablespoon red wine vinegar

1 tablespoon lemon juice

Salade Fermière
FARMER'S SALAD

The quality of the food available in the Loire is so good that it needs only the most simple of recipes to prepare it. The French have turned even this simple salad into an art form. It is substantial enough to serve on its own for lunch, with lots of French bread, but it also makes an excellent starter if served in smaller quantities – a fresh-tasting prelude to the marvellous fish, shellfish, ducks and chickens of the region. It has a marvellous combination of textures and tastes. There is a terrific range of olive oils available in most supermarkets now. If you don't yet have a favourite, I recommend an olive oil tasting. Use the nicest in the dressing for this.

Wash and dry the lettuce thoroughly and tear the leaves into pieces about the size of half a postcard. Put them into the nicest salad bowl you have. Cut the bread into small cubes about 5mm/¼ inch across. Heat the oil in a frying pan and fry the bread until just golden. Remove the croûtons from the pan as soon as they are done – they go on cooking in their own heat, and you want them crisp, not rock-like! Crumble the cheese into little bits. Mix together the vinegar, lemon juice, sugar and salt and when the sugar and salt have dissolved, add the olive oil and whisk it, beat it, stir it or blend it in a liquidizer until it is thoroughly amalgamated. Just before you are ready to serve, sprinkle the cheese over the lettuce, add the croûtons, and pour the dressing over the lot. Toss thoroughly so the dressing coats the lettuce and the croûtons and cheese are mixed in evenly.

Serves 4

1 Iceberg or crisp heart lettuce

2 slices white bread

2 tablespoons sunflower or safflower oil

50g/2oz crumbly blue cheese – Roquefort, Gorgonzola or Stilton

For the dressing:

1 tablespoon red wine vinegar

1 tablespoon fresh lemon juice

1 teaspoon sugar

½ teaspoon salt

4 tablespoons olive oil – the best you can find

Cailles en Feuilles de Vigne
QUAIL IN VINE LEAVES

Serves 4

8 quail

8 large or 16 medium-sized vine leaves

1 lemon

2 tablespoons olive oil

Although quail are classed as game, they are reared almost entirely in large enclosures in quail farms. The flavour of the vine leaves is slightly lemony, and delicious with quail.

Blanch the vine leaves in boiling water for 30 seconds, then drain them. Cut the lemon into 8 slivers lengthways and put 1 inside each quail. Rub each quail lightly with the olive oil and wrap it in vine leaves with the vein side inside. Trim off the stalk. The olive oil should help the leaves to stay on the quail, but you may need to use a cocktail stick to keep them in place.

Preheat the grill to maximum and oil the rack. Put the quail parcels on to the rack and grill them for 6–8 minutes each side. Make sure they are far enough away from the heat so the leaves do not burn, though they will dry out and go crispy in places. Serve with rice and a Cooked Pepper Salad (see p. 77).

Poule au Pot
CHICKEN IN A POT

Serves 6

1 large roasting chicken, about 2kg/4½ lb

50g/2oz fresh breadcrumbs

1 tablespoon chopped fresh parsley

1 egg

1 teaspoon freeze-dried tarragon

Optional: the liver from the chicken: you may have to ask for this as supermarkets now sell most chickens without the giblets

225g/8oz each leeks, onions and carrots

Salt and freshly ground black pepper

This is an excellent dish, and one famous for its royal connection. History is full of well-meaning slogans, and in sixteenth-century France, Henri IV, who was that rare thing, a Good King, declared that he wanted even the poorest peasants to be able to afford a chicken in the pot every Sunday. Amazingly, Henri actually managed to achieve quite a lot, and *we* have the benefits of an absolutely delicious and delicate chicken casserole, perfect for Sunday lunch or just about any other day!

Mix together the fresh breadcrumbs, parsley, egg and tarragon. If you're using it, chop up the raw liver and mix that in too. Stuff the chicken with the herby mixture. Peel the onions and carrots and wash the leeks very thoroughly. Trim the vegetables. Choose a pot into which the chicken will just fit. Put in 1 leek, ½ onion and 1 carrot and put the chicken on top. Pour in enough water to cover the chicken, season generously, add the bouquet garni and put the lid on. Bring it to the boil, then simmer very gently for 1½ – 2 hours until the chicken is tender and thoroughly cooked.

Remove the chicken and keep it warm, and throw away the cooked vegetables. Cut the remaining vegetables into pieces, add to the liquid and simmer for 10–15 minutes until they are cooked. Traditionally, the liquid would be served as a soup, with the freshly cooked vegetables sliced into it and a little fresh parsley. The stuffing can be removed and sliced into the soup, or alternatively, serve it afterwards with the chicken and fresh vegetables. You can add a few potatoes or even French bread. It's a marvellous 2-course meal from 1 pot.

Bouquet garni of
1 stick celery, 1 bay leaf,
a sprig of thyme and
4 sprigs parsley

Gratin de Courgettes
CRISPY BAKED COURGETTES

The gentle, rolling, rustic nature of the River Loire is reflected in the style of food eaten there. This is a very typical dish, simple but delicious because of the quality of the vegetables. Courgettes are marvellous eaten raw in salads, puréed into a soup, or, as here, in a gratin. This is a cheap and delicious dish, substantial enough to be served on its own.

Trim and slice the courgettes across the grain. Heat the butter in the olive oil and cook the courgettes lightly for 1–2 minutes, turning until they are just coated. Add the garlic, parsley, and marjoram or oregano, and turn for 1 minute. Pour the mixture into a gratin dish. Beat the 3 eggs together with the cream and pour over the courgettes. Top with breadcrumbs, season and bake in a medium oven at 180°C/160°C fan/350°F/Gas Mark 4, or the bottom of an Aga roasting oven, for 15–20 minutes until the top is brown and bubbling. Serve with grilled meat or fish, or just on its own with lots of crusty brown bread and butter.

**Serves 4 (or 2 as a
dish on its own)**

700g/1½lb courgettes

25g/1oz butter

1 tablespoon olive oil

1 clove garlic, peeled and
finely chopped

2 teaspoons chopped
fresh parsley

2 teaspoons fresh
marjoram or oregano,
finely chopped (or 1
teaspoon freeze-dried)

3 eggs

2 tablespoons double
cream

3 tablespoons fresh
breadcrumbs

Salt and freshly ground
black pepper

Tarte aux Abricots
APRICOT TART

Serves 6

450g/1lb pâte sablée or supermarket pastry or a bought flan case

700g/1½lb ripe fresh or good canned apricots

600ml/1 pint boiling water (for fresh apricots)

50g/2oz caster sugar (for fresh apricots)

50g/2oz apricot jam

300ml/10fl oz crème pâtissière

This uses Pâte Sablée (see p. 49) and Crème Pâtissière (see p. 135). If you're not a pastry maker, puff or shortcrust pastry from the supermarket will do very well, though the tart will not have that lovely, sweet, sandy texture of the pâte sablée.

Roll out the pastry into a large rectangle about 30 × 20cm/12 × 8 inches. Fold the outer edges in about 1cm/½ inch to make a frame for the tart. Brush the edges with a little milk and bake blind in a hot oven at 220°C/190°C fan/425°F/Gas Mark 7, or the top of an Aga roasting oven, for 15 minutes until cooked through and golden. Leave the pastry to cool.

If the apricots are fresh, dip them in the boiling water for 30 seconds. Lift them out, skin and halve them and remove the stones. Pour away all but 120ml/4fl oz of the water. Put the halved apricots into that with the caster sugar and simmer gently for 5 minutes. Do not let the apricots disintegrate. Drain and leave to cool, but keep the syrup.

If you are using canned apricots, halve and stone them if necessary. Keep just 120ml/4fl oz of the syrup from the can.

LOIRE CHEESEBOARD

The sun-washed, gently sloping hills of the Loire produce some of the finest goats' cheeses in France. Five of them have AOC status, though not all can be bought here. Those that are available make a nice cheeseboard with contrasting goaty flavours!

Valençay, which you can find here, is a nutty-flavoured goats' cheese made in Touraine. It is a soft-textured, white cheese, but dramatically dusted with charcoal, so it looks like a little black pyramid with the top cut off.

Rather stronger is Crottin de Chavignol, also available here, a white cheese with a brownish crust when it has matured for about 3 months. It then has a pleasantly sharp taste and strong smell. You can eat it when it's younger, when it is quite mild.

Two cheeses that you may have to hunt for are Chabichou – 'little goat' – which in taste and smell is unmistakably a goats' cheese! – and Selles-sur-Cher, which has a slightly less goat-like smell and a

nutty flavour that can sometimes be a bit salty.

Pouligny St Pierre is nicknamed 'the Eiffel Tower' – it looks like a rather thin pyramid, but you will probably have to go to France to find it. It too has a pronounced flavour. The texture is smooth and the rind a bluish grey.

For both the fresh and canned apricots, pour the syrup (either from cooking or from the can) into a saucepan, and add the apricot jam. Stir over a gentle heat until the jam has melted. To assemble the tart, pour the crème pâtissière into the pastry case so you have a layer about 1cm/½ inch thick. Place the apricots, cut side down, on top of the crème pâtissière in neat rows or in a pretty pattern. Using a teaspoon, carefully spread the apricot jam and syrup mixture over the tart to glaze it. If you want to, you can put the tart under a hot grill for 2 minutes to give it a slightly singed look. Allow it to set (not in the fridge) for at least 1 hour, and preferably 2–3 hours before serving.

HOW TO MAKE CRÈME PÂTISSIÈRE

This is how the French make their tarts and pies so creamy and plump-looking. When you bite into something as delectable as an apricot tart, you find hidden under the fruit this layer of rich, vanilla-flavoured creamy custard. It goes well in any tart and also in trifles and all sorts of other puds. A liquidizer or food processor makes this very easy to make.

Method:
Break the eggs into the food processor or liquidizer. Add the sugar and give it a whizz for about 15–20 seconds until smoothly blended. Then add the flour, and process again until it is well mixed in. Pour the milk into a non-stick saucepan and bring to the boil. With the motor running on the processor, pour the hot milk carefully through the feed-spout into the mixture until the whole thing is smooth. Add the vanilla essence and process for a further 5 seconds.

Scrape the mixture out of the food processor and into the saucepan, and heat very gently for about 5 minutes, stirring regularly until the mixture thickens like double (heavy) cream. Pour it into a bowl and leave it to cool, stirring occasionally to stop a skin forming on the top. Butter a piece of greaseproof paper and lay it face down on the crème, and let it cool. This keeps a skin from forming. 1cm/½ inch of this spread in a tart under apple or apricots (see p. 134) is just stunning. This will keep in the fridge, covered, for up to 3 days.

Makes 300ml/ 10fl oz

2 eggs

75g/3oz caster sugar

50g/2oz plain flour

150ml/5fl oz milk

½ teaspoon vanilla essence

PICARDY

Picardy and Flanders are also known as Le Nord, and are the parts of France closest geographically to Britain. Indeed, certain areas around Calais remained under British control until the time of the Tudors. Little trace of our linked history remains now, and the British seem to take little notice of Picardy, simply racing through it on the way south to the sunbelt. I think this is a grave mistake, since the area just beyond the channel ports has enormous charm and many hidden delights. My advice would be to avoid the temptation of taking the autoroute south immediately. The area is full of delightful little towns to explore: Montreuil-sur-Mer is one of them. The sea has long since receded more than twelve miles to the west, but the town is still surrounded by amazing sixty-foot-high defensive walls which date from the time when it was the only sea port in the whole area controlled by the King of France. Throughout the region are tiny, almost hidden, river valleys. These run through little towns with almost unpronounceable names riddled with x's and c's and h's and practically no vowels at all. But the valleys are as pretty as the names are strange. Give yourself the time to follow the back routes, to wander, and to stop at the many inns and auberges that are dotted through the region. A little attention spent on this little-visited area sometimes pays much greater dividends than joining the crowds further south.

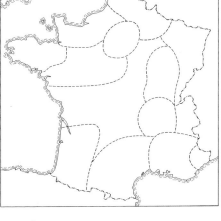

Even the ports of entry have attractions above and beyond the cheap-booze *hypermarchés* that many British people are so familiar with. Boulogne, for example, has a *haute ville*, or old fortified section, on top of a hill within easy walking distance of the ferry port. Yet it could be a different world from the one most visitors see. Boulogne is an ancient walled city with the cathedral anchoring one side and charming medieval cobbled streets and alleyways leading around an old town square. It is a beautiful town to wander around after enjoying lunch at one of the marvellous and incredibly cheap fish restaurants. Boulogne is actually the leading fishing port in the whole of France, and the range and choice of fish – both on the quayside market and in the small and occasionally grand restaurants – is quite extraordinary. Don't miss the baby mussels cooked either *marinière* or *à la crème*, or the oysters steamed in herbs in their own shells. Herrings are eaten both fresh and smoked in a way similar to our own bloaters; in Picardy they are called *craquelots* and are served

Opposite: The very pretty village of Gerberoy in the département of Oise.

with potato salad and a sprinkling of finely chopped onion.

Further inland the Flanders plains, though not visually dramatic, yield the most wonderful vegetables, in particular beetroot, leeks, turnips, carrots and potatoes, all of which are consumed with huge enthusiasm. Chicory and red cabbage are favourite vegetables in Picardy, and chicory is used in all kinds of combinations of salads and *gratins*. It is even dried and ground up to add to coffee, producing a strong, French-flavoured coffee very popular in the North. This is the part of France that shares with Belgium a passion for *frites*, the thin square chips eaten with mayonnaise as a dip – quite possibly the most cardiac-arrestingly vicious combination known to mankind! They are nevertheless extremely good chips which, when served with a steak, make one of the greatest dishes in France.

The people and the industries of Picardy have more in common with the North of England than with the South-East which lies just across the water. It is a coal-mining area, and heavy industry, centred on the town of Lille, is still a driving force. The food very much reflects this pattern, with lots of stews and slow-cooked dishes. It is also a beer region, a trait it shares with neighbouring Belgium. Another link are the *carbonards*, hearty stews named after the miners who ate them and usually made with beef or sometimes fish, layered with potatoes and cooked in a very pale light beer.

To the south lies the great champagne region based around the city of Reims. Strangely enough, champagne itself is used very little for cooking. The area's great specialities include game from the Ardennes countryside that remains one of the few great forested regions of Europe. The game is cooked in a variety of ways, sometimes in traditional hotchpots (from which we get the name hotch potch), meaning something all mixed up together – a word which must have historical connections to the hotpots of north-western Britain. Tender cuts of venison are cooked in a more modern way, grilled and with very light sauces.

Picardy is also well known for its pears. Indeed, the modern pear was first developed in France during the eighteenth and nineteenth centuries by specialist botanist/fruit enthusiasts who developed the varieties we know today, such as Williams, Bon Chrétien and Comice. As well as tasting delicious when eaten straight off the tree or with some of the local cheeses, these pears are also made into a range of tarts and pastries and are even included in some of the icecream dishes that this part of France finds so fascinating.

The people of Picardy have a taste for strong flavours, not least in the cheeses they enjoy. There is a famous cheese called Boulette d'Avesnes, named after its shape, although the rifle would have had to have been formidable. It is a blended cheese made with herbs and spices, and a very small slice provides a lot of flavour, as does another pungent cheese called Maroilles. These strong flavours don't prevent people from enjoying a wide range of pastries and cakes, including a great fondness for waffles.

If you are travelling in the area, and it is after all only a day trip away from many parts of southern Britain, it is worth bringing back some of the shellfish, particularly the tiny date-sized mussels that seem to taste so much sweeter than anything we can get on this side of the Channel. The cheeses too are worth buying, especially some of the local soft cheeses which will survive the very short journey home. In addition to its cheeses, Boulogne is also famous for its marvellous *pain de campagne* bread, made in loaves sometimes two feet across, which contain a mixture of grains – not quite wholemeal but with that special something that French bread always seems to have. As with the cheeses, the bread keeps fresh long enough to be purchased in France and eaten in Britain.

Salade d'Endives aux Oranges
CHICORY AND ORANGE SALAD

Serves 4

4 medium-sized pieces of chicory

2 large oranges, navel or similar

50g/2oz crushed walnuts (optional)

For the dressing:

2 tablespoons fresh lemon juice

½ teaspoon each sugar and salt

½ teaspoon English mustard

4 tablespoons salad oil (not olive)

Picardy is right on the Belgian border, and they are great growers of what we call chicory and they call endive – that pale, elegant pointed salad leaf. It goes amazingly well with oranges, the slight bitterness of the leaves contrasting beautifully with the sweetness of the fruit.

Rinse and wipe the chicory dry. Trim off the base and slice the chicory across the grain into 5mm/¼ inch rounds. Put these into a bowl, breaking them up slightly with your fingers to separate the rings. Peel the oranges, removing as much as possible of the white pith. Slice them in half, then slice them across the grain into 5mm/¼ inch slices as well. Remove any pips. Add the oranges to the chicory and mix gently together.

Put the lemon juice, sugar, salt and mustard into a screw-top jar and shake well, then add the salad oil and shake again until thoroughly blended. You can also whisk all the dressing ingredients together in a bowl or give them a quick whizz in a food processor or liquidizer. Pour the dressing over the salad, toss it well and allow it to stand for the flavours to develop for 15 minutes before serving in 4 pretty bowls. If you are using the walnuts, sprinkle them generously over the top.

HOW TO DEAL WITH MOULES

Serves 2 as a main course, 4 as a starter

1.2l/2 pints fresh mussels, cleaned

1 clove garlic, peeled and chopped

175ml/6fl oz apple juice, white wine or cider

Salt and freshly ground black pepper

½ cup chopped fresh parsley

Mussels are the cheapest of shellfish and very widely available. You can now buy them fresh and ready cleaned from supermarkets, and that saves a lot of hard work. In their pre-cleaned state, they require a lot of scrubbing under running water to remove the 'beards' and all the encrustations gathered from living in the sea. You still need to check the cleaned ones thoroughly, though. Put them into a bowl of clean water. Check to make sure there are no cracked shells; any that are cracked or are open, throw away. If the shells are loose, give them a slight tap. Unless they close at once, throw them away. It really is not worth taking any risks.

Moules Marinière
This is the basic mussel recipe – it means, literally, 'sailor's mussels'. From this, you can go on to add all sorts of things.

Method:
Put the cleaned mussels, garlic and apple juice, wine or cider into a large saucepan and season. Bring to the boil, cover with a lid and cook at maximum heat for 5 minutes, shaking the pan frequently. The mussels will open when cooked. Take them off the heat and throw away any mussels that have not opened. Sprinkle the mussels with the parsley and serve.

Moules à la Crème
Mussels with cream
This is my favourite mussel recipe. When the mussels have been cooked as above, take them out of the pan and keep warm. Strain the liquid and pour it back into the saucepan. Mix together 150ml/5fl oz of double cream with 2 teaspoons of cornflour until you have a smooth paste. Add this to the liquid in the saucepan and stir. Bring back to the boil, add a tablespoon of chopped fresh parsley and spoon this lovely sauce over the cooked mussels.

Maquereau au Vin Blanc
FRENCH PICKLED MACKEREL

For years Maquereau au Vin Blanc was standard on almost every French table d'hôte menu. It makes the most delicious hors d'oeuvre or light lunch, served with a salad. In France, white wine itself is used, though I prefer to use white wine vinegar for this.

Put the water, lemon juice, bay leaves, vinegar, pepper and salt into a non-aluminium saucepan. Bring to the boil and simmer for 5 minutes. Add the sliced onion, and simmer for another 3–4 minutes until the onion is translucent. Put the mackerel fillets into a baking dish and pour the hot marinade over them. Bake in a medium oven at 180°C/160°C fan/350°F/Gas Mark 4, or on the bottom of an Aga roasting oven, for 20 minutes. Take the dish out of the oven, carefully turn the fillets over, and allow them to cool in the liquid. Cover with clingfilm and keep in the fridge for 3 days before eating them.

Serves 4 as a main course, 8 as a starter

300ml/10fl oz water

Juice of 1 lemon

2 bay leaves

6 tablespoons white wine vinegar

1 teaspoon cracked black peppercorns (or coarsely ground black pepper)

1 teaspoon sea or coarse salt

1 onion, peeled and thinly sliced

8 fresh mackerel fillets

Raie au Beurre Noir
SKATE IN BLACK BUTTER

We don't seem to appreciate the fine flavour of skate in this country as much as they do in France. In fact, it is considered a great treat throughout Europe, but in Britain it is really a cheap luxury. You can serve it in many ways: with Hollandaise Sauce (see p. 118), fried, or in the classic way, with black butter.

Trim the skate wings, then put them into a large plastic bag with the flour, and shake them until they are well-coated. Heat the oil in a large frying pan, one into which all the skate will fit at once. Add half the butter and when it foams, add the floured pieces of skate. Fry over a medium heat for 4–5 minutes, turn them and fry the other side for 4–5 minutes until the skate is cooked through. Do not let the butter or flour burn.

When the skate is cooked, transfer it to warm plates. Wipe out the pan carefully with a piece of kitchen paper and add the remaining butter. Allow this to heat until it turns the colour of hazelnuts – this is known as black butter – then add the capers and pour over the skate at once. Tip the vinegar into the pan, swill it round and pour that over the skate. Serve with little new potatoes.

Serves 4

700g/1½lb skate wings, cut into 4 portions

50g/2oz plain flour

1 tablespoon oil

75g/3oz butter

1 teaspoon capers

50g/2fl oz white wine vinegar

Carbonade de Boeuf
CARBONADE OF BEEF

Serves 4

900g/2lb chuck steak

2 tablespoons oil or beef dripping

2 cloves garlic, peeled and chopped

1 onion, peeled and chopped

300ml/10fl oz beer or light beer

Bouquet garni of 1 stalk celery, 2 stalks parsley, 1 bay leaf and a sprig of thyme

1 tablespoon butter

1 tablespoon plain flour

2 tablespoons chopped fresh parsley

A carbonade is one of those dishes that crosses frontiers. As the daube is the southern French way of making a casserole, so the carbonade is the northern French way. It's based on beer. In the North of France, traditionally, they use butter, cream and beer to cook with; in the South they use olive oil, wine and garlic. A carbonade is a wonderful and quite subtle casserole.

Cut the meat into 2.5cm/1 inch cubes. Heat the oil or beef dripping in a large pan or ovenproof casserole. Put in the meat and brown it gently on all sides. That will take about 7–8 minutes, and then the gorgeous cooking beef smell starts to come through. Add the garlic and onion, and fry until they start to brown. Pour in the beer and bring to the boil. Add the bouquet garni. Cover the pan or casserole with a lid and cook in a low oven at 150°C/140°C fan/300°F/Gas Mark 2, or the simmering oven of the Aga, for 2–2$\frac{1}{2}$ hours. Stir it once during cooking to make sure all the meat remains moist.

When the meat is cooked, take the pan or casserole out of the oven. Mash the butter and flour together to make a smooth paste and add this, teaspoon by teaspoon, to the casserole, which you have put over a gentle heat on top of the stove. Allow each teaspoonful to dissolve and be absorbed in the sauce before adding the next. That, by the way, is a beurre manié, or mashed butter. Let it just come to the boil, so the sauce becomes thick and glossy and just coats the meat. Remove the bouquet garni and serve, sprinkled with chopped fresh parsley and as much mashed potato as you like!

Pommes l'Aligot
MASHED POTATOES WITH GARLIC

Substantial potato dishes are a feature of northern France. Pommes l'Aligot is a marvellous garlicky way of mashing potatoes.

Peel the potatoes and cut them up. Put them in a saucepan of water, bring to the boil and cook until tender, about 10–15 minutes depending on the size of the pieces. Drain them well and mash them together with the butter and half the warm milk. Add the garlic to the remainder of the milk in a small pan. Bring it to the boil and simmer gently for a few minutes. If you are not using the cheese, pour the garlicky milk into the potatoes and beat well until the whole lot is fluffy and garlicky.

If you are using the cheese, add it to the milk and garlic in the pan. Heat gently until the Gruyère is creamy rather than stringy. Beat it into the mashed potatoes – which will need a lot of work – until they turn into the most delicious garlicky cheesy fluffy potatoes. Serve with crusty French bread and don't disturb!

Serves 4

900g/2lb good mashing potatoes – Pentland Squire, Mafona, Kerrs Pink

40g/1½oz butter

175ml/6fl oz warm milk

2 cloves garlic, peeled and crushed

Good pinch each of salt, freshly ground black pepper and nutmeg

100g/4oz chopped or grated Gruyère cheese (optional)

Poireaux au Poêlon
LEEKS WITH LEMON AND TOMATO

A poêlon is a smallish, deep earthenware or metal frying pan, though if you do not have one, this lovely combination of leeks and lemon will cook perfectly well in an ordinary frying pan. You can serve it hot for a light lunch, with warm crusty bread, or cold as a starter.

Trim the leeks and slice them into 10cm/4 inch lengths. Wash them very well, but leave them as whole as possible. Heat the oil in a pan and fry the leeks for about 3 minutes, rolling them around so they cook on all sides. Add the tomatoes and half their juice, the lemon juice (not the rind at this stage) and sugar, and simmer gently for 15–20 minutes, stirring occasionally. Add the herbs, salt and lemon rind, turn up the heat and cook for 1 minute. Serve hot, or let the leeks cool, then chill in the fridge before serving. This will keep in the fridge for a couple of days, with the dish covered.

Serves 4

700g/1½lb leeks

3 tablespoons vegetable oil

225g/8oz canned tomatoes

Grated rind and juice of 1 lemon

1 teaspoon each sugar and salt

1 teaspoon each freeze-dried basil and oregano

Gratin de Champignons aux Pommes de Terre
MUSHROOM AND POTATO GRATIN

Serves 4

150ml/5fl oz boiling water

50g/2oz pack dried mushrooms

50g/2 oz butter

225g/8oz fresh mushrooms, finely sliced

1 onion, peeled and chopped

1 clove garlic, peeled and crushed

Salt and freshly ground black pepper

700g/1½lb potatoes, cut in 3mm/⅛ inch slices

150ml/5fl oz double cream

Grated cheese (optional)

The cooking of northern France can be hearty and robust, but the mushrooms give this gratin a subtle touch. It is a wonderful combination of golden, creamy potatoes and full-flavoured mushrooms, enhanced by the use of intensely flavoured dried mushrooms.

Pour the boiling water on to the dried mushrooms and soak for 10 minutes, then drain and reserve the water. Pat the mushrooms dry, then slice them finely. Heat the butter in a large pan, and fry the soaked and the fresh mushrooms together with the onion and garlic for 2 minutes over a medium heat. Season generously. Place half the thinly sliced potatoes in a buttered baking dish. Spread the mushroom and onion mixture over the top and then cover this with the remaining potatoes. Mix the water you soaked the mushrooms in with the double cream, and pour over the potatoes. You can sprinkle some grated cheese over the top if you like. Bake in a medium oven at 180°C/160°C fan/350°F/Gas Mark 4, or the bottom of an Aga roasting oven, for 1 hour until the sauce is bubbling and the top is golden. Serve with warm crusty bread.

PICARDY CHEESEBOARD

The pastures of Picardy produce some fine cheeses, though few are exported here. Most have strong flavours and pronounced smells.

To the south of Picardy, however, in Champagne, one of the really great cheeses is produced, one I think so stunning that I serve it on its own at the end of a meal – Chaource. It is a cows' milk cheese, with a wonderful slightly fruity flavour and deliciously creamy texture. It is round and white and delicious!

Although it is pretty well impossible to find it here, well worth trying when you are in France is Maroilles, hailed as one of the great cheeses for a 1,000 years. Its name comes from the Abbey of Maroilles where it was first made. Somewhat less aesthetically, it is also known as Old Stinky (Vieux Puant) for obvious reasons, but don't be put off. It has a fine, marvellously full flavour. The washed rind is a deep yellow-brown, and the cheese is matured for 4 months in a damp cellar.

Poires Belle Hélène
PEARS BELLE HÉLÈNE

The French have a huge taste for fancily dressed icecream, and this is one of the fanciest. Poires Belle Hélène is icecream with poached pears and chocolate sauce. The best vanilla icecream to use for this is one made with real cream and with little black flecks in it which are the bits of vanilla pod, so you know it's the real thing! If you don't have time to make the chocolate sauce, there are some good ones available. The best-shaped pears for this are either Williams or Comice, but Conference taste as good.

Peel the pears, cut them in half and take out the cores. Pour the water into a large saucepan, add the sugar and let it dissolve over a gentle heat. Add the pears, bring to the boil, then turn the heat right down and poach the pears very gently for about 10 minutes until tender, but not falling apart. Allow them to cool.

If you are going to buy chocolate sauce, make sure it is one with a good percentage of dark chocolate in it. If you are making it, melt the chocolate very gently in the cream. As it melts, add the butter and stir the whole lot together. Do not let it boil.

To serve, spoon the icecream on to 4 plates, put 2 pear halves on top of each, and pour hot chocolate sauce over the lot just before you serve it. When the hot chocolate sauce hits the icecream, it solidifies and becomes a little crunchy; when it touches the pears it stays runny, so you have this wonderful combination of flavours and textures – cold icecream, hot sauce, slightly warm pears, crunchy and runny chocolate.

Serves 4

4 large, firm, ripe pears

300ml/10fl oz water

50g/2oz sugar

225g/8oz of the best vanilla icecream you can find

For the chocolate sauce:

100g/4oz good bitter chocolate

2 tablespoons cream, single or double

25g/1oz butter, preferably unsalted

HAUTE-SAVOIE

Haute-Savoie and its neighbour, the Dauphiné, are the mountain regions in the east of France. We tend to associate this area with skiing, since both Chamonix and Grenoble are great winter sports centres with excellent facilities and superb snow. For the French, however, this part of France offers something more: it is one of the great centres for summer holidays. Time spent in the mountains is regarded as extremely healthy and the spa towns of the region, the most famous of which is Evian on the shores of Lake Geneva, have a history of visitors dating back long before the British first came to slide down hills on shaped boards.

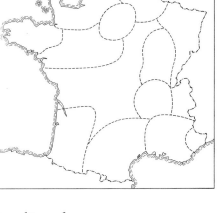

Haute-Savoie has strong connections with Italy and was part of the kingdom of Savoy throughout the late Middle Ages and much of the Renaissance. This tradition is reflected in the use of staples normally associated with Italian cooking – polenta, pasta and even the French version of ravioli, *ravioles*. The people have a reputation for hospitality and a self-sufficiency bred by life in the mountains. Many of the villages in these folded mountains are out of sight of the sun for up to 100 days a year, and in the past were entirely dependent on what they could keep and store during the winter months. They kept herds of sheep, cattle and goats, so dishes made from dairy products played a vital part in their diet – most famously the *gratin*. Historically, *gratins* were developed as sensible filling food for a harsh region, but because of their natural quality and welcome delicacy they have become the gourmet's delight. *Gratins* are always made in the same way: in a shallow dish with the principal ingredient layered with cream and flavourings and sometimes covered with cheese or breadcrumbs before being baked. There is an ongoing argument about which ingredients to include, and in particular whether cheese should be used in potato *gratins*; the general concensus is that those made in Savoie should incorporate cheese, while those made in the Dauphiné should not, but as with so many of these former peasant dishes the individual inclination of the cook should rule.

Hearty eating is very much part of the Savoie tradition. I came across an extraordinary recipe for an Easter *daube* from somewhere near Grenoble which called for half a side of beef and twenty chickens marinated in the local spirit flavoured with mountain gentian!

Opposite: Mont Granier, south of Chambéry, a dramatically-shaped peak which rises to over 6000 feet above sea level.

Escoffier, in one of his books, recalls a weekend at a country house party at the turn of the century where the hospitality was so lavish that even he felt obliged to make an excuse for his appetite. Dishes of partridge followed roast legs of mutton, which followed soups thick with whole chickens and sausages, rounded off with cheeses and fruits, and followed three hours later by a little light repast before retiring to bed.

Surprisingly, this inland part of France also has a strong tradition of fish cookery, which has evolved around the great lakes and rivers that feed it. Sadly, over-fishing has diminished the stocks to the point where the special trout and the *lombe-chevalier*, which made the region's freshwater fish famous, have become scarce and extremely expensive. New conservation and restocking are beginning to change this situation, and river fish will hopefully once again be plentiful in the area.

Cheeses are a particularly famous product of Haute-Savoie, and if you are travelling in the area you should make a point of trying some Tomme de Savoie, which is an excellent cooking cheese as well as an eating cheese. When made properly it is one of the firmer, more substantial French cheeses, coated in grape pips which give it a black and mottled appearance. A local legend has it that a young man courting a maiden in Haute-Savoie could tell how well his advances were being received by the amount of cheese she grated into his soup – the more cheese, the more passion, apparently.

Haute-Savoie is also a region to taste the waters, and there is more than one kind available. Evian is an obvious choice, but Thonon or St Simone also offer a range of flavours and mineral values. Worth looking for, too, are walnuts and some of the many products made from them: walnut oil is prized in the area around Grenoble and makes a delicious addition to salads; there are numerous walnut-based confections and liqueurs, although some of these are an acquired taste. The local walnut cakes taste delicious and travel remarkably well. They are called simply *gâteaux aux noix*.

Finally, if you have the good fortune to travel through the alpine meadows in the late summer and autumn, look out for the local mushrooms. This is probably the centre for mushroom growing, eating and gathering in the whole of France, and during the season almost every savoury dish is served with mushrooms. Whether these are ceps, field mushrooms, morels or chanterelles, the flavours, textures and intensity are quite a revelation. The most interesting and best combinations tend to be found in the small village restaurants and inns that specialize in mushroom cooking. Dishes vary from valley to valley, but it is always worth asking about them, for anyone who shows the least sign of enthusiasm is always greeted as a fellow mushroom fanatic by the inhabitants of the region.

Soupe de Broccoli au Tomme de Raisin
BROCCOLI AND TOMME DE RAISIN SOUP

The Haute-Savoie is renowned for its rich, solid, mellow cheeses, many of which it exports. This soup uses one of the best-known ones, Tomme de Raisin, a black-looking cheese coated in grape pips. It blends superbly with the subtle taste of broccoli.

Trim and chop the broccoli, and put half the florets to one side. Heat the chicken stock or water until it is boiling. Heat the oil in a large saucepan and fry the onion very gently until translucent. Add the potatoes. Stir them together, then pour in the boiling water or chicken stock and cook the potatoes and onions for about 10 minutes. Add the broccoli, season and cook until tender – about 5 minutes. Pour it into a blender or food processor with the remaining raw florets and whizz for a few seconds. The raw florets cook slightly in the heat of the soup, but give a lovely crunch to the texture. Now pour the soup back into the saucepan over a low heat. Cut the rind off the Tomme de Raisin and grate the cheese, then stir it into the soup until that lovely deep green is streaked with gold! Serve with granary or crusty French bread.

Serves 4

450g/1lb fresh broccoli

900ml/1½ pints chicken stock (a stock cube will do) or water

1 tablespoon sunflower oil

1 medium onion, peeled and chopped

175–225g/6–8oz/2 medium sized potatoes, peeled and chopped

½ teaspoon white sugar

175g/6oz grated Tomme de Raisin cheese. If you cannot find it, use Lancashire

Purée de Céleri-rave aux Pommes de Terre
PURÉE OF CELERIAC AND POTATOES

This is a very special variation of mashed potatoes. Celeriac looks a bit like a wrinkled swede, but, as its name implies, tastes wonderfully of celery. The combination is delicate and delicious.

Chop the potatoes and celeriac into 2.5cm/1 inch cubes and boil in plenty of salted water for 15 minutes. Drain well, and mash them thoroughly with the milk. Then add the butter or fromage frais and mix well – you could whisk this. Season generously.

Serves 4

450g/1lb celeriac, peeled

700g/1½lb potatoes, peeled

150ml/5fl oz milk

50ml/2oz butter or 2 tablespoons fromage frais

Salt and freshly ground black pepper

Pommes Dauphinoise
POTATOES DAUPHINOISE (IN CREAM)

Serves 4

700g/1½lb firm potatoes

1 clove garlic

50g/2oz butter

Salt and freshly ground black pepper

150ml/5fl oz double cream

150ml/5fl oz milk

This is one of the most delectable and wicked ways of cooking potatoes. If you live in the Haute-Savoie, I suppose you could be excused this excess because of the mountainous region in which you live. The rest of us will just have to live with our guilt!

You need a 4cm/1½ inch deep ovenproof dish, nice enough to serve from. Earthenware is ideal. Peel the garlic and cut it in half. Rub the dish all round with the pieces of garlic. Allow the garlic juices to dry, then rub the dish with half the butter. Wash and peel the potatoes and cut into 5mm/¼ inch slices, or use a food processor with a slicing blade. Arrange the potatoes in

---

HOW TO MAKE STOCK

Chicken stock

1 chicken carcass plus giblets if you can get them

1 onion

2 peppercorns

Pinch of salt

1.2l/2 pints water

Bouquet garni of 2 bay leaves, 2 sprigs thyme, stalks of a bunch of parsley, and the central stem of a head of celery

Vegetable stock

225g/8oz each onions and carrots

2 stalks celery with leaves

50g/2oz open mushrooms

1 clove garlic, peeled

2 tablespoons olive oil

1 teaspoon sugar

1.2l/2 pints water

Bouquet garni of 1 bay leaf, 1 sprig thyme and the stalks of ½ bunch parsley

Freshly ground black pepper and ½ teaspoon celery salt

1 tablespoon tomato purée (optional)

Good stock is an essential ingredient of a successful dish. There are some very good cubes now available, but the real thing adds an intensity of flavour to recipes that really cannot be imitated. The ingredients aren't expensive, and with chicken stock at least, it's a case of first eat your chicken . . .

Chicken stock
This also makes a marvellous soup on its own.

Method:
Put all the ingredients into a large saucepan, bring to the boil and simmer for 45 minutes to 1 hour. Strain into a large bowl. Let the stock cool, then refrigerate. The fat floats to the top, solidifies after a few hours and lifts off effortlessly.

Meat stock
Use 900g/2 lb of beef, veal or even lamb bones if you want lamb stock – the

butcher will usually give you any of these. Brown the bones for about 30 minutes in a medium oven at 180°C/160°C fan/350°F/ Gas Mark 4, or on the bottom of an Aga roasting oven, then proceed as you would for chicken stock.

Fish stock
Simply simmer fish off-cuts – heads, tails and so on, which the fishmonger will probably give you – in a large saucepan with about 1.2l/2 pints of water. Add the pared rind of a lemon, a couple of bay leaves and a couple of stalks of celery, and simmer for 45 minutes. Strain as before.

Vegetable stock
You can either use a selection of whatever you have lying around in the kitchen, or for a marvellously intense vegetable stock, use onions, carrots and

mushrooms (see Vegetable ingredients).

Method:
Peel the onions but wash and keep the peel. Peel the carrots, trim the celery and wash the mushrooms. Chop all the vegetables and the garlic finely, but keep the onions separate. Heat the oil in a large, heavy saucepan and cook the onions over a medium heat until they begin to brown. Add the sugar and stir continuously until the onions begin to caramelize and turn a dark golden brown. Don't let them burn! Put in the other chopped vegetables and the garlic and stir for 2 minutes. Add the water, the bouquet garni, pepper and celery salt and the onion skins. Cover and simmer for 50 minutes. Strain the stock and return it to the pan. If you want a thicker, richer stock, add the tomato purée.

layers in the dish, seasoning and dotting each layer with butter as you go.

When you've finished, pour over the cream and milk. Cover lightly with a piece of foil or buttered paper and bake in a moderate oven at 200°C/180°C fan/400°F/Gas Mark 6, or the top of the Aga roasting oven, for 30 minutes. Take off the foil or buttered paper and cook for a further 25–30 minutes until the top is golden brown and the whole thing deliciously bubbly and creamy. The flavour of the garlic will have gently permeated the whole dish.

Chou de Savoie Farçi
VEGETARIAN STUFFED SAVOY CABBAGE

Serves 4–6

1 large Savoy cabbage

225g/8oz onions, peeled and finely sliced

3 celery stalks, sliced

2 tablespoons olive oil

100g/4oz button mushrooms, washed and finely sliced

50g/2oz shelled walnuts, crushed

2 tablespoons light soy sauce

1 egg, beaten

175g/6oz fresh wholemeal breadcrumbs

1 tablespoon chopped fresh parsley

225ml/8fl oz vegetable stock or water

One of the favourite ways in the Savoie of serving their marvellous cabbage is to stuff it. Traditionally, the whole cabbage was stuffed, but I have to say that whenever I have tried it, the stuffing has fallen out, so this is the Crafty version!

Fry the onions and celery gently in the olive oil until soft. Add the mushrooms and walnuts. Stir it all together and fry gently for another 2–3 minutes, then stir in the soy sauce. Take the pan off the heat and add the beaten egg, breadcrumbs and the parsley to add a lovely splash of green, and mix it all together thoroughly. Take off the tough outer leaves of the cabbage, wash them and chop them up and use them to line a baking tray. Separate the rest of the leaves on the cabbage – you should have at least 12 good-sized ones – and dip each one into a large pan of boiling water. Bring back to the boil and blanch the leaves for just 30 seconds so they are easier to roll.

Take them out carefully and lay each leaf flat with the rib facing you. Place a tablespoon of the stuffing mixture on to each leaf and roll it up. The easiest way to do this is to fold over the bottom part of the leaf, then fold over the left side, then the right and roll! Lay the cabbage rolls carefully on the chopped coarse leaves in the baking tray and pour the vegetable stock or water over the top. Bake in a low oven at 160°C/150°C fan/325°F/Gas Mark 3, or the bottom of the Aga, for 40 minutes. Take them out and serve each person with 2 or 3. The mixture of flavours of walnut and mushroom and cabbage is just marvellous. You can serve potatoes or carrots with this, and, if you like, a spicy tomato sauce.

Blanquette de Veau
BLANQUETTE OF VEAL

Serves 4

700g/1½lb stewing veal cut into 2.5cm/1 inch cubes, or turkey breast or thigh

225g/8oz pickling onions, peeled (see method)

600ml/1 pint full cream milk

1 bay leaf

2 stalks celery

225g/8oz button mushrooms, washed and trimmed

1 tablespoon flour

1 tablespoon butter

Juice of ½ lemon

1 egg yolk

1 tablespoon chopped fresh parsley

The blanquette is one of the great classics of French cookery, a pale-coloured, rich-flavoured, sophisticated stew. This dish is designed for veal, but you could substitute turkey, if you prefer. Some supermarkets do now stock humanely raised veal, and if you ask for it, it may become more widely available.

The easiest way to peel pickling onions is to put them into boiling water for about 30 seconds. The skins should then slip off quite easily. Pour the milk into a large saucepan with the bay leaf and celery and gently poach the veal in it for about 30 minutes until just cooked through. Remove the bay leaf and celery and put in the mushrooms and onions. You may need to add a little water if it looks as if it is drying out. Poach for about 5 minutes until the onions and mushrooms are just cooked.

Mash the flour and butter together to make a beurre manié, and add it bit by bit to the sauce until it thickens and turns glossy. Beat the lemon juice into the egg yolk, turn the heat off and stir the yolk into the sauce – if you don't turn off the heat, the egg will scramble! Sprinkle with the parsley and serve with lots of mashed potatoes and a green vegetable.

Perdreau aux Deux Choux
BRAISED PARTRIDGE WITH TWO CABBAGES

The Haute-Savoie's reputation for excellent game precedes even its reputation for excellent skiing! Partridges are small plump birds which in season you can find at specialist game-dealers and some supermarkets. They have a fine, gamy flavour, but they are not too rich. Young birds roast very well, but older birds are delicious braised with cabbage. The best cabbage to use is, of course, a deep green Savoy.

Heat the oil in the butter in a large pan and fry the quartered partridge gently until golden on all sides. Take the partridge out and add the Dutch cabbage and onion which you have mixed together. Fry these in the partridge fat for 3 – 4 minutes until well-coated and the onion is starting to turn translucent. Add the juniper berries, caraway seeds and vinegar and season generously. Put the partridge back in the pan and pour in enough water to come just to the top of the bird. Cover the pan and simmer on top of the stove or cook in a medium oven at 180°C/160°C fan/350°F/Gas Mark 4, or the bottom of an Aga roasting oven, for 45 minutes–1 hour, depending on the size and age of the partridge.

Meanwhile, wash and cut the Savoy cabbage into 2.5cm/1 inch squares, discarding any coarse stalks. When the partridge is cooked, take the casserole off the heat, put the green cabbage on top, and return to the oven or top of the stove for 10–15 minutes until the cabbage is cooked through but still emerald-green. To serve, put some of each cabbage on to serving plates, with the partridge on top.

Serves 2

1 partridge, quartered

1 tablespoon oil

1 tablespoon butter

225g/8oz Dutch cabbage, sliced (the sort used for coleslaw)

1 large onion, peeled and sliced

2 juniper berries

½ teaspoon caraway seeds

1 teaspoon cider vinegar

Salt and freshly ground black pepper

About 250ml/8fl oz water

225g/8oz Savoy cabbage

Vegetarian Stuffed
Savoy Cabbage
(page 153)
Chicken Veronique
(page 158)

Poulet Véronique
CHICKEN VÉRONIQUE

Serves 4

4 chicken breasts

½ onion, peeled and stuck with 2 cloves

2 bay leaves

2 fresh parsley stalks

300ml/10fl oz unsweetened white grape juice

2 teaspoons cornflour

Juice of ½ lemon

150ml/5fl oz single cream

175g/6oz muscat grapes, halved and de-seeded, or use seedless white grapes

Salt and freshly ground black pepper

The grapes give a clear sweetness to this classic dish, which is very quick and easy to cook. Muscat grapes are available in summer, and have easily the best flavour, otherwise use seedless green grapes – don't use red grapes in this recipe.

Place the chicken breasts in a casserole or saucepan with the onion and herbs and cover with the grape juice. Put the lid on and simmer for 20–25 minutes until the chicken is thoroughly cooked. Remove the onion and herbs and throw them away. Place the chicken breasts on a warm serving dish. Blend the cornflour and lemon juice together. Stir into the cream, then whisk into the cooking liquid in the pan over a medium heat until you have a thick, smooth sauce. Add the grapes and just heat them through for 1–2 minutes, no more. Adjust the seasoning, then pour the sauce over the chicken breasts and pile the warm grapes around the chicken.

HAUTE-SAVOIE CHEESEBOARD

The high, mountainous pastures of the Haute-Savoie are full of cheesy treasures, some of which are readily available here and make a fine cheese-board.

One of these is Reblochon, which also happens to be one of my favourite cheeses. It is shaped like a flattish disc, with a reddish-pink rind, and is a rich creamy cheese with a marvellously full but unaggressive flavour.

Tomme de Savoie is a semi-hard cheese. There are 24 Tomme cheeses, and 9 of them come from Savoy. Tomme de Savoie is made from cows' milk and is pale gold in colour with a darkish rind. Its pronounced smell belies a very pleasant, nutty flavour.

We tend to think of the lovely, nutty-flavoured Gruyère as solely a Swiss cheese, but there is a French version which is produced in the Savoie,

and also just to the north in Franche-Comté.

One of the best cheeses from the Savoie, which is not available here, is Beaufort. It is a fine, fruity-tasting cows' milk cheese, firm textured and pale gold coloured and much admired by cheese connoisseurs.

Poires aux Amandes
PEAR AND ALMOND PUDDING

The flavour of pears and almonds together is just wonderful, and this is also a spectacular-looking pudding, particularly if you make it in individual soufflé dishes.

Peel the pears, then halve and core them. Put them in a saucepan with enough water just to cover them and add the caster sugar and vanilla essence. Poach them gently for 5 minutes. Take the pears out of the syrup and allow them to cool. You can use the syrup on another occasion for fruit salad.

Mix together the ground almonds, flour and soft brown sugar. Whisk the eggs with the milk and beat into the flour and almond mixture until you have a smooth batter. Put the pears in a buttered china soufflé or flan dish, or individual buttered flan or soufflé dishes, and pour the almond mixture over the top. Smooth down and bake in a medium oven at 190°C/170°C fan/375°F/Gas Mark 5, for 30–35 minutes until the almond mixture is fully risen, set and golden on top, flecked with brown. Do not let it brown too much, but make sure it is cooked through. Slide a skewer into it, and if it comes out clean, the pudding is done. Serve immediately with a little pouring cream.

Serves 4

2 large Comice or Williams pears, not too ripe

25g/1oz caster sugar

½ teaspoon vanilla essence

100g/4oz ground almonds

50g/2oz self-raising flour

75g/3oz soft brown sugar

3 eggs

180ml/6 fl oz milk

Savoie au Citron
SAVOY LEMON SPONGE CAKE

The pâtisserie of the Savoy is famous throughout France. This lemon sponge cake is typical of the region, light and fragrant.

Grate the rind of half the lemon and finely chop all of the remaining half, including the skin. The Crafty way to make this cake is in a food processor. Put all the ingredients into the food processor and whizz for 10–15 seconds. Scrape down the sides and whizz again. If you want to make it by hand (which is much slower), cream together the butter and vanilla sugar. Beat in the eggs, then add the lemon and the flour.

Place the mixture in 2 × 18cm/7 inch round tins and bake for 25 minutes in a medium oven at 180°C/160°C fan/350°F/Gas Mark 4, or the bottom of an Aga roasting oven. Allow them to cool, then take them out of the tins.

To make the lemon butter cream, cream together the butter and sugar. Add the lemon juice and rind and whip until light. Sandwich the cakes together with the lemon butter cream and decorate with lemon icing. Alternatively, use lemon marmalade as the filling, and decorate with a little sieved icing sugar.

Serves 4

1 lemon

175g/6oz softened butter

175g/6oz vanilla sugar

3 eggs

175g/6oz/1¼ cups self-raising flour

For the lemon butter cream:

175g/6oz butter

100g/4oz caster sugar

Juice and grated rind of 1 lemon

THE NIÇOIS

The Niçois is a small region centred on the town of Nice, close to the border of Italy. Indeed, it was only in the nineteenth century that the Comté of Nice became an official part of France. It still fiercely maintains its own identity and even possesses its own language, Nissart, although sadly this is a dying tongue spoken only by older people. Nice itself, however, has by and large succeeded in resisting the homogenization of the Riviera that growing popularity caused during the last century. With its sister towns of Monte Carlo and Cannes, Nice in the late nineteenth century saw the arrival of the super-rich, the establishment of casinos to cater for them, and the influx of celebrities like César Ritz, the Swiss hotelier, who with his friend and comrade in cuisine Auguste Escoffier helped to set the standards for grand hotels and grand living in the area.

Nevertheless, Nice still maintains its links with an older age. Many of its culinary traditions go back to medieval times when the town was part of the kingdom of Savoy, connected to Italy rather than France. Indeed, some of the flavours can be traced even further back, to the Greeks and Romans. It is believed that the Greeks first colonized the area now known as Antibes, and perhaps it was they who made olives, and in particular black olives, such an intrinsic part of Niçois tradition. If you are travelling in this region, do go down to the old town of Nice and look around the grocers where the range of olives has to be seen to be believed. They travel well in their little plastic tubs or pre-packed cartons and, along with oil and soap, are the best mementoes of the area to buy and bring home. Another staple of Niçois cuisine is the anchovy: not only are they in plentiful supply, they are also used in the most extraordinary range of dishes.

Together with olives, anchovies produce one of the definitive Niçois dishes, *pissaladière*. Despite the similarity in name with the Italian pizza, and although both are based on bread dough with added flavourings, *pissaladière* evolved quite separately: 'Pissalat' is an ancient combination which can be traced back to Roman times. Anchovies and sardines were chopped up finely with herbs and left to rest for a month or so until they started to ferment. This mixture was then spread on to bread dough along with olives, onions and other flavourings. Today *pissaladière* can be made quite simply with tinned anchovies – the same as those that the Niçois add to casseroles of beef

Opposite: One of the most beautiful coastlines of the Côtes d'Azur, Esterel Corniche lies between St Raphael and Cannes.

and to a famous spread called *tapenade*, to which black olives and capers are also added.

The flavours and foods in the Niçois are strong and vivid, very similar to its western neighbour, Provence. It is an area of plentiful melons and peaches, herbs and garlic, and those wonderful, deep red, misshapen tomatoes that always taste three times as delicious as any others. It is also very strongly dependent on fish, and tuna has long been a central catch of the fishermen along this part of the coast. Tuna is becoming scarcer now, as a result of the over-fishing that has been going on for so long, but it remains a vital ingredient of one of the other great Niçois dishes: *salade niçoise*. A dish that excites as much passion as any in France, *salade niçoise* has a devoted following of 'experts' who regard it as totally wrong if made without their particular combination of olives, anchovies, eggs, tuna and tomatoes. The addition of ingredients like potatoes and green beans, lettuce, fennel or even cucumber is a cause for almost lifelong rage, with columns of newspapers devoted to the argument year after year. I believe that the balance of a good *salade niçoise*, made with any one of the combinations authenticated by various traditions, is one of the great pleasures of any French summer.

Although we often forget the fact, there is a winter in this part of the world too. It doesn't bring snow and ice but it does bring cold and rain, with driving winds, and this is reflected in some of the lesser-known but warming dishes based on salt cod and pulses such as chickpeas and haricot beans. There is also a strong tradition – not always maintained these days – for thickening sauces with bread rather than with egg yolk or flour particularly in some of the strong garlic-flavoured condiments that are used in fish soups.

Another Niçois speciality eaten by the locals is *trochia*, a kind of baked egg mixture sold in slices like a savoury cake. It is made with chard or spinach, herbs, eggs and Parmesan cheese from over the border in Italy. The cheeses around Nice tend to be soft, made to be sold and eaten quickly. It is not an area famed for its pâtisserie either, but at Christmas this all changes, when the famous *treize desserts*, eaten on Christmas Eve before attending Midnight Mass, are brought out. This feast traditionally includes nuts and fruits (usually crystallized or preserved); sweetmeats like nougat; baked pastries like rather grand biscuits; and in the centre a *pompe*, a yeast cake made with brown sugar and candied peel; and confits made of flavoured sugar. In the more traditional families these are preceded by a meal based on salt cod, as Christmas Eve is a *maigre*, or meat-free, day. The desserts are left out all over Christmas for people to pick at, as they don't require refrigeration to keep them fresh.

Salade Niçoise

Food in this part of France is just full of the sun. It is easy to cook these recipes throughout the year, as most ingredients are now available all the time. Obviously they are better eaten on a vine-shaded terrace, sometime in mid-July with the Mediterranean lapping at your toes – but these recipes cheer you up wonderfully wherever you are! Salade Niçoise is *the* great classic salad. I often eat it as a main course with French bread, with perhaps some cheese and fruit to follow.

Wash the potatoes, but don't peel them, and wash and trim the beans. Boil the potatoes for about 6 minutes in plenty of water in a big pan. After 6 minutes, add the beans and the eggs (to hard boil them) and boil the whole lot for about another 8 minutes. By that time, the potatoes should be cooked, the beans should be bright green and still a bit crunchy and the eggs should be just cooked through. Put the whole lot into a colander and run cold water over them for about 2 minutes. It stops everything cooking and keeps the beans fresh. Shell the eggs and cut each into 4, then start arranging the salad.

Wash and dry the lettuce and tear it into quite small pieces. Arrange it in a large, quite shallow bowl. Wash the tomatoes, halve them if they are the baby ones, or cut into quarters if they are bigger, and put them in a ring round the edge. Arrange the potatoes in a ring – you may have to cut them in half, unless they are really small, then the eggs inside that, then the beans in a ring, so you now have a series of wonderful concentric circles. Into the middle of that you pile the slightly broken-up tuna. Separate the anchovies and arrange in a decorative pattern over the salad – a lattice design looks very effective. Add the olives. Pour the oil from the anchovy can over the whole thing.

To make the dressing, mix together the lemon juice, sugar and salt, then add the oil and whisk until thickened and thoroughly blended. Pour all the dressing over the salad no more than 5 minutes before you serve it. Serve with hot crusty French bread.

Serves 4

225g/8oz/6 small new potatoes – one of the salad varieties

225g/8oz little, stringless green beans

4 eggs

1 Webb's Wonder or Cos lettuce

225g/8oz tomatoes, preferably tiny cherry tomatoes

1 can tuna fish, about 175g/6oz, drained

1 can anchovies, preferably in olive oil, about 50g/2oz

At least 5 or 6 black olives, or as many as you like!

For the dressing:

2 tablespoons fresh lemon juice

½ teaspoon sugar

½ teaspoon salt

4 tablespoons olive oil

Rouget Grillé
GRILLED RED MULLET

Serves 4

4 red mullet, each about 175–200g/6–7oz

4 tablespoons olive oil

4 tablespoons fresh lemon juice – that's about 1½ lemons

Salt and freshly ground black pepper

4 large bay leaves

1 fennel bulb with all the feathery bits on

A handful chopped fresh parsley

1 lemon, sliced

You no longer have to wait to go to southern parts to eat fish such as red mullet. It is now widely available in this country. It is a very good fish to eat – it is dense, solid and very filling. The Niçois region is influenced by Italian cooking – Italy is, after all, just next door – but it has a distinct cooking style of its own. This is a classically simple dish. If you do have difficulty finding red mullet, trout is a good alternative.

Put all the fish into a glass or china bowl, pour the olive oil and lemon juice over them, season with the salt and pepper, and marinate for at least 30 minutes and anything up to 6 hours. You can leave it up to 12 hours in the coldest part of the fridge, covered in clingfilm.

When you are ready to cook them, stuff each fish with a bay leaf and the feathery green bits which you have cut off the fennel. Line the grill pan with silver foil. It doesn't affect the taste, but it does improve the washing up! Wash the fennel and slice it finely, arrange it in a layer over the foil, and put the mullet on top. Drizzle a little of the marinating oil and lemon juice over the fennel slices and red mullet. Preheat the grill to maximum and cook the fish for 5 minutes each side until the skin is crisp and the flesh cooked through. Put the red mullet on to warm plates. Stir the fennel and all the juices from the pan together and pour a couple of tablespoons on to each plate. Put a slice or 2 of lemon and a little chopped parsley on top. Serve this with rice, or sautéed potatoes.

Bar au Safran
SEA BASS IN SAFFRON SAUCE

Sea bass is a marvellous white fish, with a delicate flavour and texture. It is very much a special occasion fish, not only because of its fine flavour, but also because it is very expensive. You can substitute a small, whole salmon, which also goes very well with the lovely golden saffron sauce.

Line a baking dish with a lightly oiled sheet of kitchen foil and sprinkle it with a little salt. Sprinkle some more salt into the cavity of the fish and stuff with the parsley sprigs and bay leaves. Grate the rind from 1 of the limes (set this aside) and squeeze the juice of both of them over the fish. Bake in a medium oven at 180°C/160°C fan/350°F/Gas Mark 4, or the bottom of an Aga roasting oven, for 45–50 minutes until the fish is just done. You can, if you like, turn it once, halfway through the cooking time.

Transfer the fish to a serving dish and ease off the skin from the top. Pour the cooking juices into a non-stick saucepan, add the cream, saffron and lime rind, and bring to the boil. Simmer for 5 minutes until the sauce is thick. If the sauce does not thicken enough, mix a heaped teaspoon of cornflour with a little water, remove the sauce from the heat, and stir in the cornflour paste. Put it back on the heat and stir until the sauce is thick and glossy. To serve, carefully separate the fish fillets at the table, and coat each serving with the sauce.

Serves 4

1 sea bass or whole salmon, about 1.25kg/2½lb

Sea or coarse salt

2 sprigs fresh parsley

2 bay leaves

2 limes

180ml/6fl oz double cream

¼ teaspoon ground saffron

1 teaspoon cornflour (optional)

Bouillabaisse Michael Barry
MY BOUILLABAISSE

Serves 4

450g/1lb fish: choose 3 kinds from red mullet, gurnard, haddock, coley, rock salmon and hake

4 tablespoons olive oil

225g/8oz onions, peeled and finely chopped

2 cloves garlic, peeled and finely chopped

1 stalk celery, finely chopped

2 bay leaves

Small bunch fresh parsley, stalks separated and leaves chopped

500ml/17fl oz passata

400ml/14fl oz fish stock (see p. 152)

Pinch of saffron strands (optional)

2 tablespoons chopped fresh parsley

Croûtons

Grated Gruyère cheese

Rouille (see p.16)

Bouillabaisse in its traditional form is almost impossible to make in this country: we just do not get the right selection of fish. It is also very time-consuming and painstaking to prepare. This is a delicious, simplified version, made with readily available fish, but still full of the flavours of the Mediterranean. Ask the fishmonger to skin the fish, and ask also for some fresh fish trimmings for the stock.

Heat the oil in a large pan and sauté the onions, garlic, celery, bay leaves and parsley stalks for 5 minutes. Add the passata and fish stock, bring to the boil, then simmer for 10 minutes. Cut the fish into neat pieces not more than 5 × 2cm/ 2 × 1 inches. Add them to the soup and simmer gently for 5–7 minutes until the fish is thoroughly cooked. If you are using saffron strands, steep them in a tablespoon of hot water for 1 minute, then add to the saucepan. Stir the soup gently, so the fish pieces don't break up, and serve sprinkled with parsley. Offer bowls of croûtons, grated Gruyère cheese and Rouille.

Pissaladière
ONION FLAN NIÇOISE

Pissaladière is the Niçois version of pizza. Its name is *not* derived from pizza, but from a local condiment called pissalat, which is anchovy purée mixed with herbs, spices and olive oil. It isn't that easy to find pissalat in this country, but a tin of anchovies does very well. Apart from anchovies, pissaladière is also a wonderful excuse to eat lots and lots of onions.

Mix the yeast and sugar together with a little of the warm water and leave it for about 10 minutes until it is frothy. Mix in the remainder of the water together with the other bread dough ingredients – the flour, ascorbic acid, olive oil and salt – and knead it into a firm dough. Spread the dough on a greased baking tray that is at least 30cm/12 inches square, and leave it to rise. The ascorbic acid makes the dough rise in 12–15 minutes, a quarter of the time it would normally take.

While the dough is rising, fry the onions gently in the olive oil until soft. When the dough is ready, spread the onions thickly on top, then arrange the anchovies on that in a criss-cross pattern and dot with the black olives. Bake for 20 minutes in a hot oven at 210°C/190°C fan/ 425°F/Gas Mark 7, or the top of an Aga roasting oven, until the dough is cooked through and the onions are a marvellous golden colour.

Serves 4

For the bread dough:

15g/½oz/about 2 teaspoons fresh yeast

Pinch of sugar

300ml/10fl oz warm water

450g/1lb strong or bread flour

Pinch of Vitamin C powder (ascorbic acid)

2 tablespoons olive oil

1 teaspoon salt

For the topping:

700g/1½lb onions, peeled and sliced

2 tablespoons olive oil

1 can anchovies

12 black olives

Noisettes d'Agneau à la Purée d'Ail
LAMB NOISETTES WITH GARLIC SAUCE

Tender lamb and a subtle garlic sauce make this one of my favourite dishes. In southern France, garlic can be used as a predominant, powerful flavouring, as in rouille. Here it is used as a delicate, creamy sauce.

To make the sauce, put the diced potato into a pan with the crushed garlic. Add the milk, and simmer gently, uncovered, for 15 minutes, or until the potato is soft. Blend, process, or push through a sieve to make a smooth sauce.

Heat the oil in a heavy frying pan until very hot. Fry the noisettes with the rosemary for about 2 minutes each side, a little more if you like the meat well-cooked. Season when ready. Pour the sauce on to a serving dish and arrange the noisettes on top. Serve with little green beans or a green salad.

Serves 4

8 lamb noisettes

1 King Edward potato, peeled and diced

4 cloves garlic, peeled and crushed

300ml/10fl oz milk

2 tablespoons oil

½ teaspoon freeze-dried rosemary

Salt and freshly ground black pepper

Boeuf Niçois
BEEF CASSEROLE NIÇOIS

Serves 4

900g/2lb stewing beef or shin of beef

4 tablespoons olive oil

225g/8oz onions, peeled and chopped

3 cloves garlic, peeled and chopped

2 tablespoons tomato purée

Water, red wine, or my favourite, red grape juice (for quantity, see method)

Piece of orange peel

Bouquet garni of 1 stalk celery, 2 stalks parsley, 1 bay leaf and sprig of thyme

50g/2oz black olives

This is a variation on the daube – the southern French slow-cooked casserole. It is full of the flavours of the South, some expected, others less so – oranges, olives and garlic.

Cut the beef into 3cm/1½ inch cubes. Heat the olive oil in a large pan or casserole and sauté the beef on all sides until it starts to brown. Add the onion and garlic, and cook for a couple of minutes until the onion begins to turn translucent. Stir in the tomato purée and pour in enough water, red wine or red grape juice to come to the top of the beef. Add the orange peel and bouquet garni and simmer in a low oven at 160°C/150°C fan/325°F/Gas Mark 3, or the bottom of the Aga simmering oven, for 1½–2 hours, depending on the cut of meat. When the meat is tender, take out the peel and bouquet garni and stir the olives into this rich, dark dish. Serve with flat noodles.

NIÇOIS CHEESEBOARD

Like the rest of Provence, cheese from this south-eastern corner does not travel well, and apart from Banon you are unlikely to find cheeses from here in Britain. Your Niçois cheeseboard will have to be supplemented by goats' cheese from other regions, or even some Dolcelatte from across the border in Italy.

The local cheeses are well worth trying if you visit the Riviera. Brousse, for example, is a curd cheese made from ewes' milk, which is just as happy served with herbs and garlic as it is served with sugar, fruit and cream, while Cachat is a smooth, mild, creamy cheese made from either goats' or ewes' milk.

Tomates Grillées à la Niçoise
GRILLED TOMATOES NIÇOISE

Tomatoes in southern France are superb, and this is a simple dish which sets them off to perfection. You need giant beef or Marmande tomatoes, weighing up to 450g/1lb each, generously seasoned and grilled until the top is almost black. You can serve these as a starter, or as a light main course with warm French bread and some cheese, preferably goat's cheese, to follow.

Cut the tomato in half and place both halves, cut side up, in a shallow, heatproof, earthenware dish. Score the cut sides with a sharp knife in a criss-cross pattern, to allow the flavours to penetrate. Mix the crushed garlic and salt together and spread equal amounts on each tomato half. Sprinkle the parsley and breadcrumbs over the top, then drizzle $1/2$ teaspoon of olive oil over each half. Pre-heat the grill for at least 5 minutes, then grill the tomatoes under a high heat for 10 minutes until the top is crispy and black. Serve at once.

For each person:

1 beef or Marmande tomato

1 clove garlic, peeled and crushed

½ teaspoon salt

1 teaspoon finely chopped fresh parsley

1 teaspoon fresh breadcrumbs

1 teaspoon olive oil

HOW TO MAKE REAL CUSTARD AND CRÈME BRÛLÉE

Crème brûlée is a marvellous creamy custard and one of the great, classic dishes. Whether or not it is actually French is open to some dispute. There is a recipe for this dish in an early Cambridge manuscript, where it was called Burned Cream. I suspect it was a universal dish over much of Europe. It came into fashion when sugar became available in serious quantities in the seventeenth century. Wherever it comes from, the French have turned crème brûlée into one of their greatest dishes.

Method:
In a saucepan, heat together gently the double and single cream, the caster sugar and vanilla essence and the milk, until the sugar has dissolved. Bring it just to the boil, then turn off the heat and leave to cool.
Blend the cornflour mixture and whisk it into the cooled cream mixture together with the eggs and egg yolks. Strain the mixture into 6 heatproof bowls or soufflé dishes and put them in a baking tin. Pour a little water into the tin to come 2.5cm/1 inch up the sides of the dishes. Bake in a medium oven at 180°C/160°C fan/350°F/

Gas Mark 4, for 20 minutes or until the custard is firm. This is delicious, just as it is.
To make crème brûlée, melt the granulated sugar with the water in a non-stick saucepan until it goes pale gold in colour and smells like toffee. Make sure it doesn't burn. Allow the caramel to cool for 3 minutes, then pour over the custard in the dishes. Leave it to set, but don't refrigerate or the caramel will go soggy.

Serves 6

300ml/10fl oz/1¼ cups double cream

150ml/5fl oz single cream

75g/3oz caster sugar

½ teaspoon vanilla essence

150ml/5fl oz milk

½ tablespoon cornflour, mixed with 2 tablespoons water

3 eggs

3 egg yolks

100g/4oz granulated sugar

2 tablespoons water

INDEX